Late Victorian House Designs

56 American Homes and Cottages with Floor Plans

D. S. Hopkins

Dover Publications, Inc.
Mineola, New York

Bibliographical Note

This Dover edition, first published in 2004, is an unabridged republication of the work originally designed and published by D. S. Hopkins, Architect, Grand Rapids, Michigan, in 1893 under the title *Houses and Cottages, Book No. 7: A Collection of House and Cottage Designs / Containing 57 [sic] Designs Costing from $1,600 to $2,500.* The double-page spreads from the original oblong book have been redesigned so that the house, floor plans, and text are on the same page. The original frontmatter has also been reformatted in a similar way.

Library of Congress Cataloging-in-Publication Data

Hopkins, D. S. (David S.)
    [Collection of house and cottage designs]
    Late Victorian house designs : 56 American homes and cottages with floor plans / D.S. Hopkins.
       p. cm.
    Originally published: Houses and cottages, book no. 7 : a collection of house and cottage designs, containing 57 [sic] designs costing from $1,600 to $2,500. Grand Rapids, Mich. : D.S. Hopkins, 1893.
    ISBN 0-486-43593-8 (pbk.)
    1. Architecture, Domestic—United States—Designs and plans. 2. Architecture, Victorian—United States—Designs and plans. I. Title.

NA7207 .H66 2004
728'.37'0973—dc22

                                          2004041358

Manufactured in the United States of America
Dover Publications, Inc., 31 East 2nd Street, Mineola, N.Y. 11501

WHAT IS IN MY FOUR BOOKS?

To the Building Public:—

The popularity and demand for my published designs call for another and larger edition of my books. In this edition I have a large variety of styles and costs, classified into four books including 104 new designs, never published before. Book 6, contains 58 designs, ranging from $150 up to $1,500 and includes all styles and manner of plans, all practical and of the latest style of enclosure. The study has been to produce good looks by good proportions and plain, tasty details. No sawed work, ginger bread styles, but all substantial and lasting. Book 7, contains 57 designs costing from $1,600 up to $2,500. All styles imaginable. All practical and tasty. Several double tenement designs. Book 8, contains 54 designs costing from $2,600 to $3,500; all modern in plan and arrangements. Quite a number of double tenements shown in this book. Book No. 9, contains 20 designs of dwellings, costing from $3,600 up to $10,000, and 12 designs of stables, ranging from $150 up to $1,500. In these books will be found the greatest variety and styles of plans published. Price, $1.00 for any single book; any two books, $1.50; all four, $2.00; postage prepaid. Any party purchasing books and ordering plans from same, will be credited with cost of same on said plans.

THE BENEFIT OF PROCURING PLANS, WORKING DETAILS, ETC.

With proper plans it is an easy matter to build a satisfactory house, and if the architect furnishes such, he will repay the amount of his fees many times in the sense of security given the client as well as the builders, as both will know just what is to be done before commencing, and the owner will receive what he pays for.

All drawings must be plain and explicit on all points involved in the construction, and with the full and complete specifications combined, would protect the owner's and builder's interests alike. Many builders have the idea that plans are only for the owner's interest. This is a great mistake. To the honest builder plans and specifications are of the utmost importance, and are his safeguard oftimes, regarding his reputation, etc.

Only One Right Way to Build. And first when about to build study up ideas and take plenty of time to satisfy yourself of your wants, requirements, etc., and then when you get your plans, have them right just as you wish the house to be built. The exterior part you have to leave largely to the architect, as that is what he is for—to clothe up and dress the building suitably and in good taste, and at the same time substantially. Avoid these freaky styles; best to depend upon good proportions and pleasing roof lines, and particularly upon the proper coloring in painting or staining of the building. The plans in these books can all be changed or modified to suit, and patrons will be assisted cheerfully in making any selections, and pencil sketches, etc., will be sent back and forth until the client is fully satisfied, when the orders are properly placed, as under head of "How to Order Plans." It is not the intention to confine patrons to these plans in any respect and charge for every slight change. Any interior change such as moving partitions, putting in or taking out a fire place, moving doors or windows, so long as you do not disturb the exterior, no extra charge is made; but when changes require enlarging or reducing size of plans or change in height of stories, such changes would require new elevations and extra charges, as near actual cost as possible would be made.

Competition is the best and only way to get the best figures and is only possible when you have complete plans, details and specifications, from which all can figure alike.

No plans are kept in stock, except the original office copies, and from one to three days or a week is required, from the time of receiving the final order to get out the full plans. But if time is limited the foundation plan can be prepared at once and forwarded so work can be commenced.

PRICES FOR PLANS.

If you find a design in this book that pleases you as it is, the price given on page 10 is for full plans, full size details, and complete specifications and bill of materials, all very full and complete, so any ordinary carpenter or builder will have no trouble in going ahead and completing the work, and in case you do not find just what you want, write me what changes you desire made, first placing your order and complying with conditions given on next page (How to Order Plans, Etc.), and I will scale up a plan with changes and send to you for approval.

———— · ☉ · ————

NEW WORK. Where you have an idea of your own that you have studied up for floor plans and you would like full plans from same, I will be pleased to work them out, submiting pencil sketches, and giving full satisfaction, the same as if from any of my designs. My charges for new meritorious work would be about two per cent. upon cost of buildings. If the design was out of the usual order, as to general wants, the charges would be two and one-half per cent. upon the cost of building.

———— · ☉ · ————

THE PLANS.

The elevations of at least three sides of building, and necessary floor plans and foundation plan are drawn to a scale of $\frac{1}{4}$ inch to one foot upon tracing cloth, all neatly bound up in a neat waterproof cover. The roof and frame plan gives all sides of building, showing pitch of roofs, height of studding and stories, and all materials pertaining to framing the frame properly.

The exterior details are all drawn full size, that will go on paper 36 inches wide, and 7 feet long. All interior details are full size or large scale drawings. Doors and stairs are all given in full size and scale details.

Knowing as I do that my working drawings when they leave the office, go out of reach of my personal supervision, I have taken especial pains to make everything very plain and easily understood by the builders. Every exterior detail that goes from the office is full size and drawn by hand (not printed).

The specifications are very full and complete, giving all minute instructions, how to do all work, and the kind and size of materals, kind and size of nails to use for certain places, quality of material, glass, hardware, plumbing, tinning, colors for painting, with color cards, in fact all and every particular concerning constructing the building complete. Rules governing contractor, if let by contract, and bill of material if required; also a set of blank builder's contract ready for filling out.

———— · ☉ · ————

HOW TO ORDER PLANS, AND WHAT I DESIRE TO KNOW.

After having decided to have certain plans, or some one changed to suit you, observe the price given, and send with your order at least one-third of cost of said plan, as a guarantee of good faith, and pencil sketches will be sent for approval, as before mentioned when desired, free of charge when the above conditions are complied with. Where full price of plans is sent with order, the plans are sent express paid. Otherwise plans when complete will be sent C. O. D. collect return charges, with privelege of examination at express office. Make all remittances for plans by draft, express, or money order (do not send individual checks), payable to the order of D. S. Hopkins, on the receipt of which your order will receive prompt attention.

———— · ☉ · ————

PARTICULAR.

I desire patrons to be very particular about informing me regarding the plumbing (if wanted included), also sewerage, gas, water supply, cesspool, door hardware, kinds of woods for finish for different rooms, stone or brick foundations; how much cellar, furnace, water or steam heat, shingle, slate or metal roof, and any particular matter not usual about such building.

REGARDING ESTIMATES.

As it is impossible to make estimates that will hold good in all parts of the country where prices of material and labor vary so much and facilities for getting mill work done are not good, in consequece, home prices have been used, as given below. The lowest estimate given is based upon these figures, and for the higher estimate 25 to 30 per cent. has been added, which will be sufficient for almost any locality where materal and labor are not too high.

PRICES AS USED FOR ESTIMATING.

Excavation, per yard,	$ 20
Stone foundation put in complete, per perch (26 cubic feet)	2.25
Brick laid in wall, per M,	12.00
Plastering, two coats, per yard,	.20
Frame lumber, per M, Hemlock,	11.00
Flooring ready to lay, per M,	17.00
Siding, second clear, 4 inch, ready to lay, per M,	16.00
Sheeting and roofing, per M,	12.00
Pine shingles, per M, best 16-inch sawed,	3.00
Slate, best laid per square (100 ft.),	8.00
Finished lumber, pine, per M,	30.00 to 35.00
Painting, per yard, each coat,	.06
Carpenter's wages, per day,	2.25
Mason's wages, per day,	3.50
Laborer's wages, per day,	1.50
Hardwood, finished (with hardwood doors extra over pine), per room, about	20.00

INCLUDED IN THE ESTIMATES.—

For small cottages with brick foundation, 9 inch walls are used; for larger houses, 12 inch walls; where stone is used for foundation 16 inch walls for small, and 18 inch walls for larger wood residences; for brick dwellings heavier walls are used in proportion to size, etc. In nearly every case the walls show 2 feet 6 inches above grade or finish. Dressed or matched sheeting with water-proof building paper under weather boarding and exterior finish is included in all estimates. Roofs to be boarded tight for slate and paper lined under, and open roofing for shingles, no paper.

Brick work for chimneys, good even colored hard burned brick for ordinary work, others good pressed brick. All outside doors 1¾ inches thick, and all glass double strength, A. A. American Sheat; good quality of hardware; heavy tin gutter and conductors; for ordinary cheap work, galvanized iron conductors, for the better grade of work, all tin work. Porch floors, ⅞ inch by 4 inch, paint joints, three coats of paint. A cistern is included, also cement bottom and banks in all cellars. No mantels, hearths, grates or heating are included in estimates. If plumbing is estimated, description of designs will mention it.

THE MODIFICATIONS.

These are suggestions showing some of the many changes that could be made if desired on each design. Always bear in mind that any change that requires new drawings will be charged extra for in proportion to time required in making same. The estimated cost does not include any of these modifications.

Prices of various fixtures, etc., which will assist patrons to determine the extra cost of changes. Supposing water and sewerage to be within 25 to 30 feet of the house. To connect with water main and carry to sink in lead pipes with sill cock for lawn sprinkling $20 to $25, and in connection provide 30 gallon galvanized iron boiler and bath room with wash out tank water closet, wash bowl with hot and cold water and 10 ounce copper-lined bath tub with hot and cold water, all complete with neat nickle fixtures, if not over 30 feet from range or stove, $115. Without boiler or hot water $80. Gas piping from $10 to $25. Hot air furnace from $100 to $250. Steam, $300 to $500; hot water, $400 to $800, as a bases, double the price for hot water over steam ordinarily, double price of furnace for steam. Mantels, grates and tile hearths cost from $25 up. A neat design with over mantel and bevel glass miror costs from $50 to $75, in all ordinary natural wood finish. Cesspools cost from $10 to $25. Bay windows and small porches from $40 to $75. Seventy-five barrel cistern, brick lined and arched $25 to $30.

PRICE-LIST

OF

Full Plans, Full Size Details and Specifications

FOR ALL THE DESIGNS IN THIS BOOK.

PLANS, AND HOW TO ORDER THEM, SEE PAGE IV.

No. 144,	$28.00	No. 44,	$33.00	No. 49,	$40.00
No. 43,	33.00	No. 146,	33.00	No. 51,	40.00
No. 172,	28.00	No. 45,	35.00	No. 53,	40.00
No. 91,	30.00	No. 147,	33.00	No. 54,	40.00
No. 155,	28.00	No. 46,	30.00	No. 56,	40.00
No. 38,	25.00	No. 148,	28.00	No. 58,	35.00
No. 97,	30.00	No. 48,	30.00	No. 64,	35.00
No. 95,	40.00	No. 50,	35.00	No. 92,	30.00
No. 100,	28.00	No. 154,	40.00	No. 29,	30.00
No. 39,	25.00	No. 52,	35.00	No. 140,	28.00
No. 108,	28.00	No. 132,	35.00	No. 169,	25.00
No. 40,	30.00	No. 75,	35.00	No. 180,	28.00
No. 113,	30.00	No. 36,	33.00	No. 181,	35.00
No. 26,	30.00	No. 37,	30.00	No. 182,	30.00
No. 125,	30.00	No. 33,	30.00	No. 186,	30.00
No. 41,	28.00	No. 32,	30.00	No. 187,	30.00
No. 133,	28.00	No. 31,	33.00		
No. 156,	25.00	No. 21,	30.00		
No. 42,	30.00	No. 27,	30.00		
No. 145,	30.00	No. 30,	35.00		

There are parties who do not wish to pay so much for their plans to build from, so I have concluded to offer blue print work on heavy paper where I usually use hand tracings and give parties their choice between hand tracings or blue prints. This blue print work can only be used when design is taken as shown in books, that is there cannot be any changes made upon the plans, as the prints are made from the original tracings only. All changed plans will have to be hand traced. Drawings can be reversed in blue prints.

These drawings are just the same in every particular as the hand tracings, only that they are on paper considerably heavier than the paper in this book, and are just as good to build from as the tracings. The only difference is they will be about worn out by the time the house is completed, which is all that is generally desired of a set of drawings, or at least is all you can expect of the details and other drawings. With the exception of the scale drawings of floor and foundation plans and the elevations, the drawings are precisely alike in every particular, with specifications, details, bills of material, etc., and I can furnish them at 25 per cent. or one quarter less in price.

A FEW VALUABLE TABLES FOR THOSE WHO ARE BUILDING.

16 Cubic Feet   equal 1 cord–foot.

8 Cord feet or }

128 Cubic feet } equal 1 cord.

24½ Cubic feet....1 perch of stone or masonry.

A perch of stone is 16½ feet long, 1½ feet wide and 1 foot high. Stone masons usually call 25 cubic feet one perch.

By the square, means 100 square feet, as in plastering, flooring, slating, shingling, etc., and is 10 ft. square, surface measure.

Eight hundred shingles averaging 4 inches wide, laid 4½ to weather will cover a square.

A cistern averaging 8 feet deep and 8 feet in diameter will hold 95 barrels of water. One averaging 6 feet 6 inches in diameter and 6 feet 6 inches deep will hold 51 barrels of water.

ESTIMATES OF MATERIALS.

3½ barrels of lime will do one hundred square yards plastering, two coats.

2 barrels of lime will do one hundred square yards of plastering one coat.

1 bushel of hair will do one hundred square yards of plastering.

1¼ yards good sand will do one hundred square yards of plastering.

⅓ barrel of plaster (stucco) will hard finish one hundred square yards plastering.

1 barrel of lime will lay 1,000 brick. (It takes good lime to do it.)

2 barrels of lime will lay one cord rubble stone.

½ barrel of lime will lay one perch rubble stone (estimating ¼ cord to perch).

To every barrel of lime estimate about ⅝ yards of good sand for plastering and brick work.

Five pounds of 4d or 3¾ pounds of 3d nails will lay 1,000 shingles. 5¾ pounds of 3–penny nails will put on 1,000 lath. In lathing one bundle of lath and 184 nails will cover 5 yards.

1,000 lath will cover 70 yards of surface and 11 pounds of 3 penny nails will nail them on. 8 bushels of lime, 16 bushels of sand and 1 bushel of hair will make enough good mortar to plaster the same.

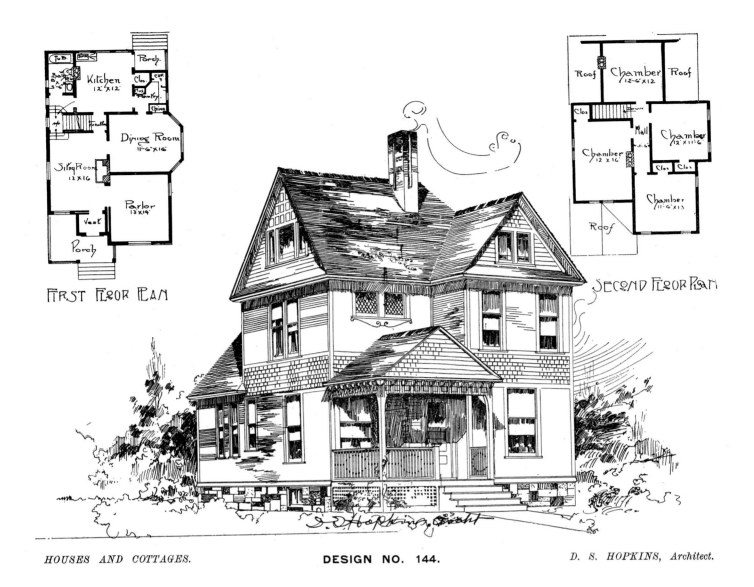

FIRST FLOOR PLAN

SECOND FLOOR PLAN

HOUSES AND COTTAGES.   DESIGN NO. 144.   D. S. HOPKINS, Architect.

DESIGN NO. 144.

FRAME two-story cottage. Size 29x44 feet, over all. This is a little, cozy common-sense cottage. This study is one of economy, convenience and pleasantness. Height of stories: First, 9 ft.; second, 8 ft. 6 in. Stone foundation, cement, bank shelf cellar under entire house, 7 ft. deep. First and second story sides clapboarded, with shingle belt over first story windows. Shingle gables and roof.

First story contains vestibule, 4x5 feet 8 inches; sitting room, 12x16 feet, with fire place; dining room, 11 feet 6 inches by 16 feet; kitchen, 12x12 feet, with closet; pantry, 7x8 feet, and bath room, 5 feet 6 inches by 8 feet. This bath room is so arranged that it can be used by up stair occupants as well as by the family generally, and makes the plumbing much less expensive. Double acting stairs.

Second story contains front chamber, 11 feet 6 inches by 13 feet; side chamber, 12x16 feet; opposite side chamber, 11 feet 6 inches by 12 feet, and rear chamber 12x12 feet 6 inches. Closets, rear and front porches.

MODIFICATIONS: Stone cellar under entire house; fire place in chamber of second floor. Fire place could be put in dining room if desired.

Estimate cost as here shown—no plumbing, mantels, grates or heating, pine finish, $1,500 to $1,800.

See price list for cost of full plans, page vi.

The lowest estimate of cost is in accordance with price list of material and labor as given on page v, and by comparing with your local prices you can ascertain the cost of any of these buildings in your vicinity.

For changing shingles to clapboards on exterior of any design or reversing of plans, no extra charge will be made.

1

HOUSES AND COTTAGES.

DESIGN NO. 43.

D. S. HOPKINS, Architect.

DESIGN NO. 43.

FRAME two-story dwelling and attic. This makes a pleasant, home-like looking house. Size 30x48 feet all over. Height of stories: First, 10 feet; second, 9 feet 6 inches. Cellar under whole house 7 feet deep. Stone foundation from cellar bottom. Sides clapboarded; gables, fancy battens and shingle roof.

First story contains vestibule, 5x7 feet 6 inches; parlor, 13x15 feet; sitting hall, 12x16 feet, with alcove fire place; dining room, 12x15 feet 6 inches, with fire place; kitchen, 11x12 feet; pantry, 5 feet 6 inches by 11 feet. Front and rear porch, back and front stairs.

Second floor contains front chamber, 13x15 feet, with balcony off from same; side front chamber, 11 feet 6 inches by 12 feet; side chamber, 11x12 feet; bath room, 5x12 feet; servant's room, 11x12 feet 6 inches, and attic stairs. All pine finish. No plumbing, mantel, grates or heating.

MODIFICATIONS: Fire place could be placed in chamber of second floor. Balcony could be enclosed in with front chamber, and another small chamber worked in by taking some off from each of the front chambers. End sitting hall can be square if preferred.

Estimate cost as here shown, $1,800 to $2,400.

See price list for cost of full plans, page vi.

The lowest estimate of cost is in accordance with price list of material and labor as given on page v, and by comparing with your local prices you can ascertain the cost of any of these buildings in your vicinity.

For changing shingles to clapboards on exterior of any design, or reversing of plans, no extra charge will be made.

2

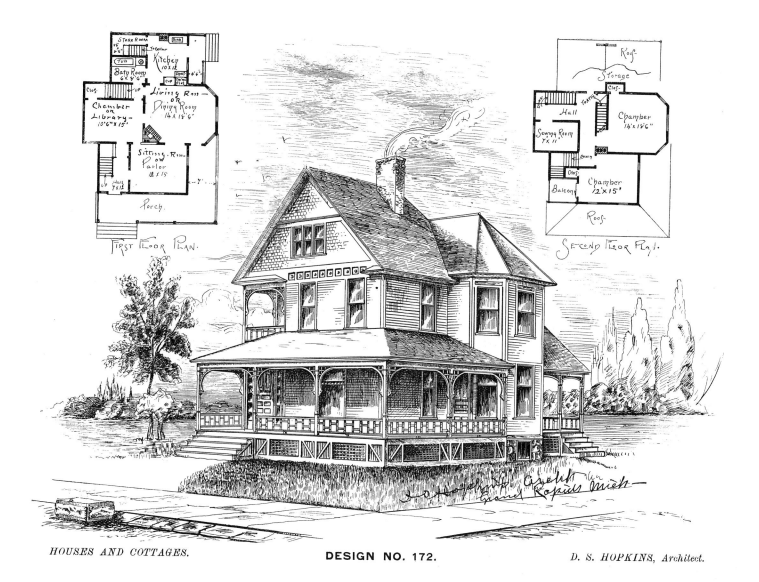

HOUSES AND COTTAGES.   DESIGN NO. 172.   D. S. HOPKINS, Architect.

DESIGN NO. 172.

FRAME two-story cottage. Size 35x47 feet all over. A cheap, common–sense cottage. Just room enough for comfort. The idea is to live in the whole house or "what is good enough for the visitors is good enough for me." Height of stories: First, 9 feet 6 inches; second, 8 feet. Stone or brick foundation. Walled cellar under the rear part 7 feet deep. First and second stories clapboarded, gables shingled. Shingle roof.

First story contains entrance and stair hall, 7x12 feet; sitting room or parlor, 12x15 feet; dining or living room, 14x18 feet 6 inches, with fire place; library or chamber, 10 feet 6 inches by 15 feet, with closets; bath room 6x8 feet 6 inches, convenient for all parts of house; kitchen, 10x12 feet; store room, 5 feet 6 inches by 8 feet 6 inches; china closet, cupboards, etc., side and front porch, front and rear stairs.

Second story contains front chamber, 12x15 feet, with door to balcony; one side chamber, 14x18 feet 6 inches, with closet; servant's chamber or sewing room, 7x11 feet, and storage room under wing room; also stairs to attic.

MODIFICATIONS: Cellar under entire house. Rear part carried up so as to get another chamber or two upon second story. A room could be built on back for kitchen, and present kitchen used as dining room if desired.

Estimate cost as here shown, pine finish and plumbing, no mantels or grates, $1,500 to $1,800.

See price list for cost of full plans, page vi.

The lowest estimate of cost is in accordance with price list of material and labor as given on page v, and by comparing with your local prices you can ascertain the cost of any of these buildings in your vicinity.

For changing shingles to clapboards on exterior of any design or reversing of plans, no extra charge will be made.

3

First Floor Plan.

Second Floor Plan.

HOUSES AND COTTAGES,   DESIGN NO. 91.   D. S. HOPKINS, Architect.

DESIGN NO. 91.

TWO STORY frame cottage. Size, 40x45 feet over all. This makes nice resort cottage having plenty of porches, balcony, etc., with large rooms and fire-places in all principal rooms. The design is so that cooking is done outside of cottage. Set on posts or piers. Height of stories: First, 10 feet 6 inches; second, 9 feet 6 inches. First story clapboarded, second story shingled. Shingled roof.

First story contains wide porch on front and one side; one parlor, 13 feet 6 inches by 15 feet; one 15x17 feet; dining room, 13 feet 6 inches by 25 feet 6 inches, the three latter have fire-places; hall 10x16 feet, with stair case; pantry 7x8 feet and rear porch 7x18 feet.

Second floor contains four chambers, closets, balcony, etc. All pine finish. No mantels, grates or hearths.

MODIFICATIONS: This design can be enlarged if desired and culinary addition or kitchen, etc., built on back if required with porch between. A bath room can be arranged for upon second floor with some slight changes. Estimate cost as here shown, $1,200 to $1,600.

See price list for cost of full plans, page vi.

The lowest estimate of cost is in accordance with price list of material and labor as given on page v, and by comparing with your local prices, you can ascertain the cost of any of these buildings in your vicinity.

For changing shingles to clapboards on exterior of any design or reversing of plans, no extra charge will be made.

DESIGN NO. 155.   *D. S. HOPKINS, Architect.*

DESIGN NO. 155.

FRAME two story cottage. A convenient, inexpensive dwelling. Size, 27x43 feet over all. Height of stories: First, 9 feet 4 inches; second, 9 feet. Stone foundation. Cement shelf bank cellar under dining room and kitchen, 7 feet deep. First story sides clapboarded. Second story sides and gables shingles. Shingle roof.

First story contains reception room, 12x14 feet; sitting room, 13 feet 6 inches by 14 feet (with fire-place); dining room, 12x14 feet 6 inches and fire-place; rear porch entrance; china closet; kitchen, 11 feet 6 inches by 12 feet and pantry 5x11 feet; kitchen porch; front porch 7x12 feet; enclosed stairs; double acting and to cellar under same.

Second story contains front chamber (with bay), 12x13 feet; front chamber 12x13 feet; chamber 12x12 feet, and one 9x13 feet, closets to each.

MODIFICATIONS: Height of stories can be changed. Open stairs can be arranged in réception hall with a little change of roofing. A bath room can be had on second floor over pantry. Estimate cost as here shown, all pine finish, no mantels, grates or heating, $1,500 to $1,800.

See price list for cost of full plans, page vi.

The lowest estimate of cost is in accordance with price list of materal and labor as given on page v, and by comparing with your local prices, you can ascertain the cost of any of these buildings in your vicinity.

For changing shingles to clapboards on exterior of any design or reversing of plans, no extra charge will be made.

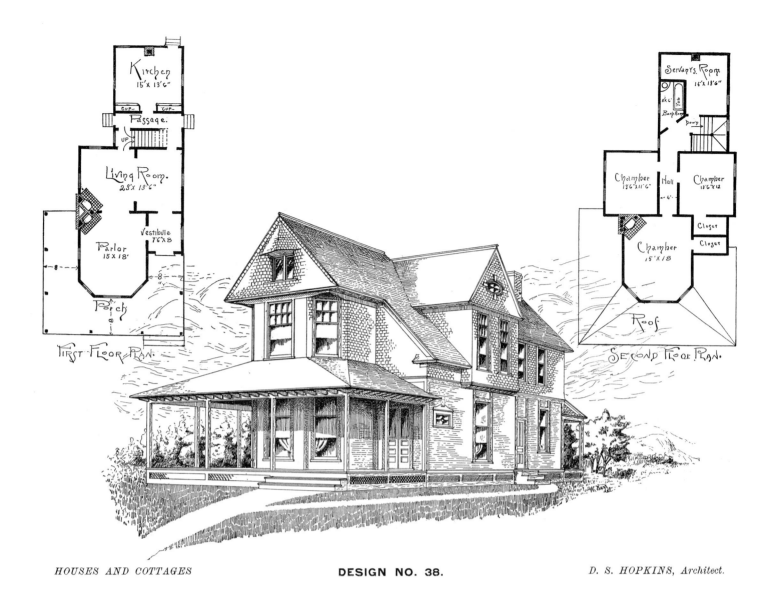

HOUSES AND COTTAGES   **DESIGN NO. 38.**   *D. S. HOPKINS, Architect.*

DESIGN NO. 38.

FRAME two story Southern style of house. Size, 32x64 feet including porch 8 feet wide. Height of stories: First, 11 feet; second, 10 feet. No cellar. Set on posts or piers. First story clapboarded. Second story and gabels shingles. Shingle roof. This is a house with plenty of wide porch.

First story contains vestibule, 7 feet 6 inches by 8 feet; parlor, 15x18 feet (with fire-place); living · room, 13 feet 6 inches by 23 feet (with fire-place). This room can be divided into two with portiers cutting off dining room part from the other, if desired. Stairs and open passage between living room and kitchen. Kitchen, 13 feet 6 inches by 15 feet, with cupboards, etc.

Second story contains three good-sized chambers, hall, bath room and servant's room with closets. All pine finish. No plumbing or mantels.

MODIFICATIONS: Could have a foundation put under same. Another fire-place can be provided in chamber second floor. By enlarging vestibule, front stairs could be put in if desired. Sliding doors could be put in place of the portiers. Estimate cost as here shown, $1,300 to $1,700.

See price list for cost of full plans, page vi.

The lowest estimate of cost is in accordance with price list of material and labor as given on page v, and by comparing with your local prices you can ascertain the cost of any of these buildings in your vicinity.

For changing shingles to clapboards on exterior of any design or reversing of plans, no extra charge will be made.

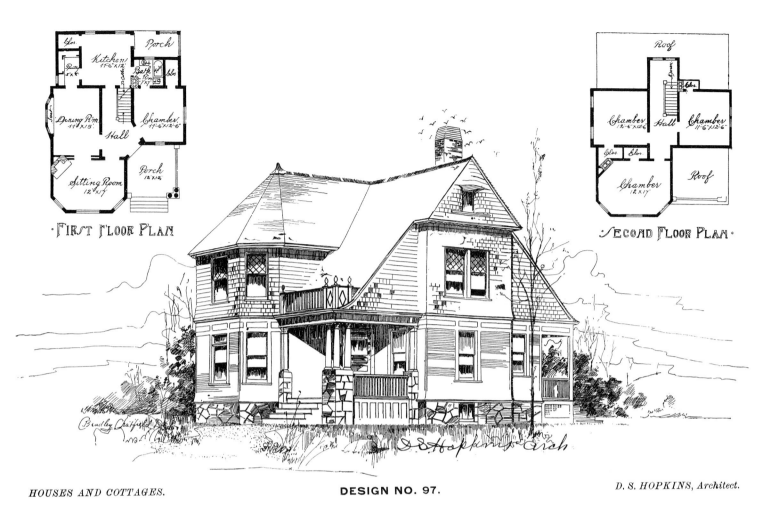

HOUSES AND COTTAGES.   **DESIGN NO. 97.**   *D. S. HOPKINS, Architect.*

DESIGN NO. 97.

FRAME two story cottage. A design many will be pleased with, as it has a chamber and bath room upon first floor and is arranged for comfort. Size, 32x42 feet over all. Height of stories: First, 9 feet; second 8 feet 6 inches. Stone foundation and cellar under the rear portion of house. Stone to cellar bottom 7 feet deep. First story sides clapboarded. Second story and gables shingles. Shingle roof.

First story contains stair hall, 7x15 feet (with open stair case); sitting room, 12x17 feet (with fire-place); dining room, 11x15 feet; chamber, 11 feet 6 inches by 12 feet 6 inches, with closet and bath room 6x7 feet; kitchen, 11 feet 6 inches by 12 feet, with closet and pantry, 5x8 feet 6 inches; front porch, 12x12 feet, and kitchen porch, 6x11 feet.

Second story contains front chamber, 12x17 feet; chamber, 12 feet 6 inches by 12 feet 6 inches; chamber, 11 feet 6 inches by 12 feet 6 inches, and closets to all.

MODIFICATIONS: House could be enlarged by building a kitchen and pantry on rear and use the present kitchen and pantry for dining room. A fire-place could be placed in dining room and chamber over sitting room if desired. Lavatory could be arranged upon second floor. Estimate cost as here shown with hardwood finish in principal rooms first floor, balance pine, with plumbing, no mantels, grates or heating, $1,950 to $2,300. Deduct for plumbing, $150.

See price list for cost of full plans, page vi.

The lowest estimate of cost is in accordance with price list of material and labor as given on page v, and by comparing with your local prices you can ascertain the cost of any of these buildings in your vicinity.

For changing shingles to clapboards on exterior of any design or reversing of plans, no extra charge will be made.

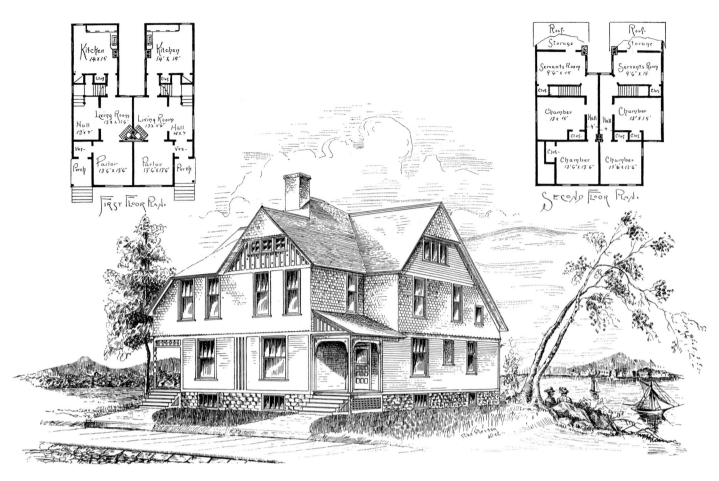

Kitchen
14x15

Kitchen
14' X 15'

Clos

Clos

Living Room
13 x 16

Living Room
13' x 16'

Hall
13' x 7'

Hall
13'X 7'

Ves-

Ves-

Porch

Parlor
13'6"x13'6"

Parlor
13'6"x13'6"

Porch

FIRST FLOOR PLAN.

Roof
Storage

Roof
Storage

Servants Room
9'6" x 15

Servants Room
9'6" x 15

Clos

Clos

Clos

Clos

Chamber
13' x 15'

Hall
4'

Hall
4'

Chamber
13'X15'

Clos

Clos

Clos

Clos

Chamber
13'6"x 13'6"

Chamber
13'6"x 13'6"

SECOND FLOOR PLAN.

HOUSES AND COTTAGES.   **DESIGN NO. 95.**   *D. S. HOPKINS, Architect.*

DESIGN NO. 95.

FRAME two-story double tenement house. Size 40x42 feet over all. The idea of this tenement is to get the actual comforts of a house in as economical a way as possible for small families. Height of stories: First, 9 feet; second, 8 feet 6 inches. Stone foundation. Cellar under all main part 7 feet deep. First story clapboarded; second story shingled, gables paneled and shingled. Shingle roof.

First floors contain front porches, entrance vestibule, with doors into parlors or halls. Parlors, 13 feet 6 inches by 13 feet 6 inches; living rooms, 11 feet 6 inches by 13 feet (with fire places); halls, 7x13 feet, with stairs starting from same and also kitchen stairs join the main stairs on landing out of sight from halls, which has two doors between same and kitchens. Kitchens, 14x15 feet, with cupboards, sink, closets and cellars.

Second floors contains three good-sized chambers with closets. All pine finish. No mantels, grates or heating.

MODIFICATIONS: Not many modifications can be made on such a cheap double tenement. Second story rear might be carried up so as to get a bath room in front of servant's room and move same back, or two small chambers could be made of the space.

Estimate cost as here shown $1,800 to $2,300.

See price list for cost of full plans, page vi.

The lowest estimate of cost is in accordance with price list of material and labor as given on page v, and by comparing with your local prices, you can ascertain the cost of any of these buildings in your vicinity.

For changing shingles to clapboards on exterior of any design or reversing of plans, no extra charge will be made.

8

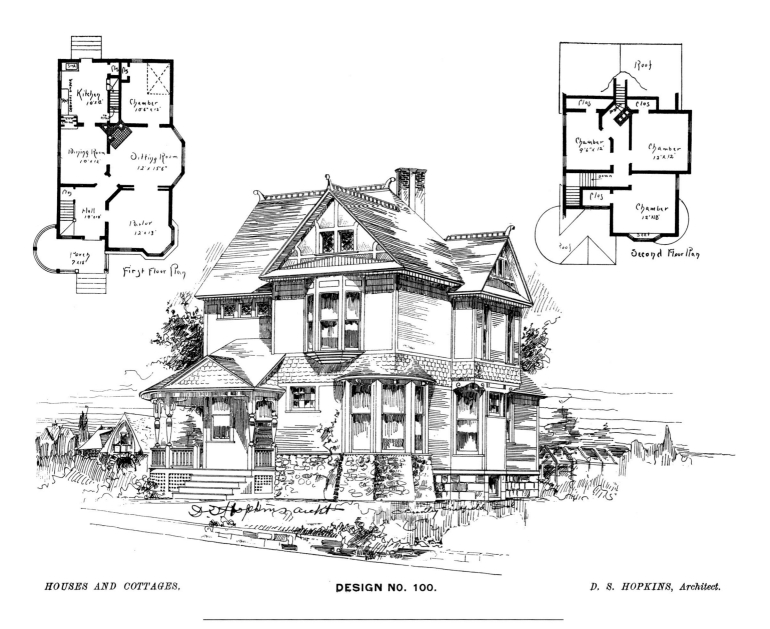

First Floor Plan

Second Floor Plan

DESIGN NO. 100.

FRAME two-story cottage. Size 31x43 feet over all. This design, I think, contains as much room and convenience as can be had for the cost. Height of stories: first, 9 feet; second, 8 feet 6 inches. Cellar under the four rear rooms. Stone foundation and cellar 7 feet deep. Sides clapboarded, except shingle belt between first and second story windows. Gables ceiled and paneled. Shingle roof.

First story contains hall, with stair case, 10x10 feet; parlor, with corner bay, 12x13 feet; sitting room, 12x15 feet 6 inches, with fire-place; dining room, 10x12 feet; chamber, 10 feet 6 inches by 12 feet; kitchen, 10x12 feet; rear and cellar stairs, cupboards and china closets.

Second story contains front chamber 12x13 feet, with bay; one back, 12x12 feet, and one 9 feet 6 inches by 12 feet, with closets.

MODIFICATIONS: Rooms can be enlarged. Hardwood for all principal rooms on first floor in place of pine. Pantry can be placed between the kitchen and dining room by projecting back kitchen, width of pantry, which would require kitchen chimney. Extra rear kitchen porch. A large bath room can be placed in attic over kitchen, and hall provided to get to same at an expense not exceeding $50 extra, aside from plumbing. By raising up the rear half story another chamber and bath room could be arranged for, or two chambers.

Estimate cost of the cottage as here shown is from $1,600 to $2,000—pine finish, no mantels, grates or heating.

See price list for cost of full plans, page vi.

The lowest estimate of cost is in accordance with price list of material and labor as given on page v, and by comparing with your local prices you can ascertain the cost of any of these buildings in your vicinity.

For changing shingles to clapboards on exterior of any design, or reversing of plans, no extra charge will be made.

HOUSES AND COTTAGES. DESIGN NO. 39. D. S. HOPKINS, Architect.

DESIGN NO. 39.

FRAME two-story southern style house. Size 35x46 feet, including front porch 8 feet wide. Height of stories: First, 11 feet; second, 10 feet. No cellar. Set on posts or piers. First story sides clapboarded; second story shingles or clapboards; gables shingled. Shingle roof. This design is strictly a southern or summer house. It' has high ceilings and good sized rooms; plenty of fire-places; large porches, one a dining porch; kitchen entirely disconnected from any main part rooms.

First story contains center hall 8x18 feet, with stairs off from same; living room, 15x18 feet, with fire-place; parlor, 12x15 feet, with fire-place; large portiers from both living room and parlor into hall, so virtually are all one room if so desired; kitchen, 12x15 feet; pantry, 6x10 feet, and dining porch, 12x18 feet 6 inches, with fire-place. Enclose this in with a wire screen and it will make a delightful porch for various purposes.

Second story contains three chambers of good size; bath room and servant's room, with closets, etc. Pine finish. No plumbing.

MODIFICATIONS: The open porch dining room can be enclosed in same as other part of house if desired. Three more fire-places can be put up stairs in chambers if required. Porch can be extended down one side if case requires.

Estimate cost as here shown, $1,400 to $1,600.

See price list for cost of full plans, page vi.

The lowest estimate of cost is in accordance with price list of material and labor as given on page v, and by comparing with your local prices, you can ascertain the cost of any of these buildings in your vicinity.

For changing shingles to clapboards on exterior of any design or reversing of plans, no extra charge will be made.

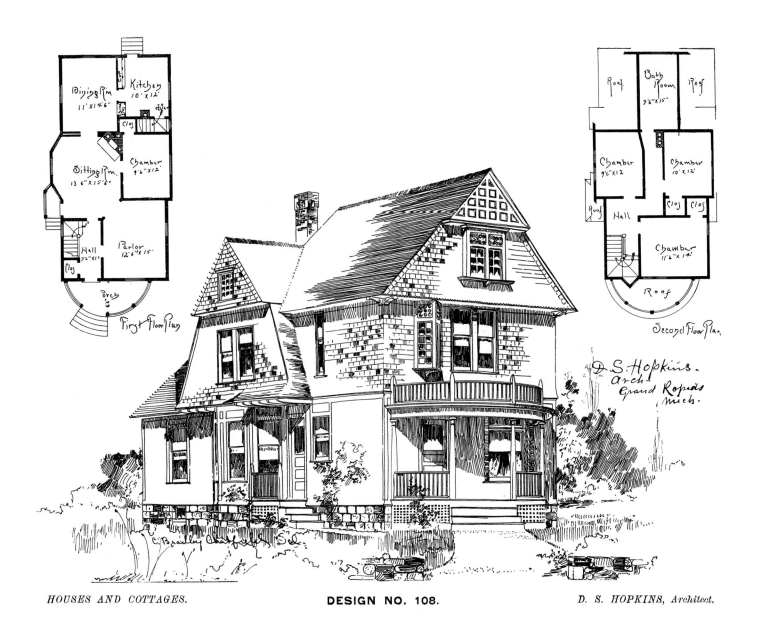

HOUSES AND COTTAGES.   **DESIGN NO. 108.**   *D. S. HOPKINS, Architect.*

DESIGN NO. 108.

FRAME two-story dwelling. Size 24x50 feet over all. Height of stories: first, 9 feet; second, 8 feet 6 inches. Cellar under rear half of house. Stone foundation and cellar 7 feet deep. First story sides clapboarded; second story and gables shingles. Shingle roof.

First story contains hall and open stair case 7 feet 6 inches by 11 feet; parlor, 12 feet 6 inches by 15 feet; sitting room, with bay and fire-place, 13 feet 6 inches by 15 feet 6 inches; chamber, 9 feet 6 inches by 12 feet, with closet; dining room, 11x14 feet 6 inches; kitchen, 10x12 feet; china closets, cupboards, etc. To cellar from kitchen. Front porch 7x16 feet, and side-covered entrance to sitting room.

Second story contains front chamber 11 feet 6 inches by 14 feet, and side chambers 9 feet 6 inches by 12 feet, and 10x12 feet, with closets and bath room 7 feet 6 inches by 15 feet over rear part.

MODIFICATIONS: Enlargement of general plan. Cellar under whole house. Rear part carried up another story and one more chamber provided for, and rear stairs from kitchen to second floor.

Estimate cost as here shown, no plumbing, mantels, grates or heating, pine finish, $1,450 to $1,800.

See price list for cost of full plans, page vi.

The lowest estimate of cost is in accordance with price list of material and labor as given on page v, and by comparing with your local prices you can ascertain the cost of any of these buildings in your vicinity.

For changing shingles to clapboards on exterior of any design or reversing of plans, no extra charge will be made

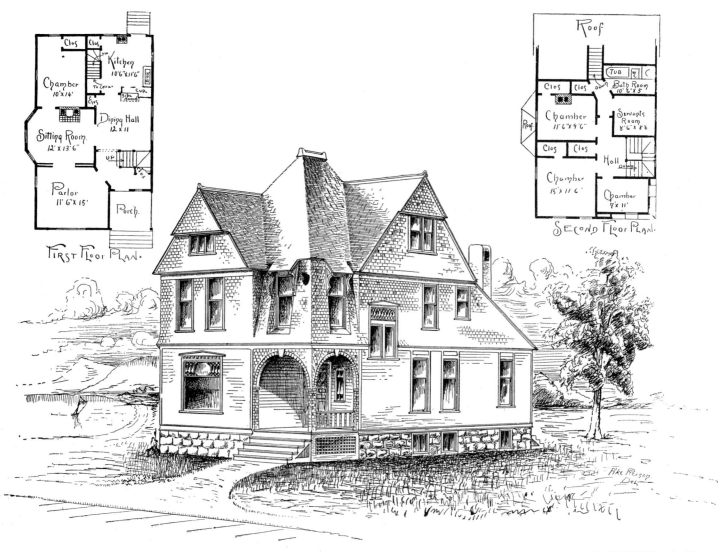

First Floor Plan.

Second Floor Plan.

HOUSES AND COTTAGES.   DESIGN NO. 40.   D. S. HOPKINS. Architect.

DESIGN NO. 40.

FRAME two story cottage. Size, 27x40 feet. Height of stories: First, 9 feet; second, 8 feet 6 inches. Stone foundation and cellar under whole house, 7 feet deep. First story sides clapboarded; second story and gables shingled. Shingle roof.

First story contains stair hall or entrance, 8x12 feet, thrown into dining room (by beam overhead and grille finish), which is 11x12 feet; parlor, 11 feet 6 inches by 15 feet; sitting room, 12x13 feet 6 inches (with fire-place); chamber, 10x14 feet, with closet; kitchen, 10 feet 6 inches by 11 feet 6 inches, with closet, cupboards, etc. Back stairs.

Second floor contains four chambers, closets and bath room. All pine finish. No plumbing, mantels or grates.

MODIFICATIONS: House could be generally enlarged if required. Rear part can be carried up another story and two more chambers provided. Plumbing costs $175. Three principal rooms and hall in hardwood add $75. Estimate cost as here shown, $1,600 to $2,100.

See price list for cost of full plans, page vi.

The lowest estimate of cost is in accordance with price list of material and labor as given on page v, and by comparing with your local prices, you can ascertain the cost of any of these buildings in your vicinity.

For changing shingles to clapboards on exterior of any design or reversing of plans, no extra charge will be made.

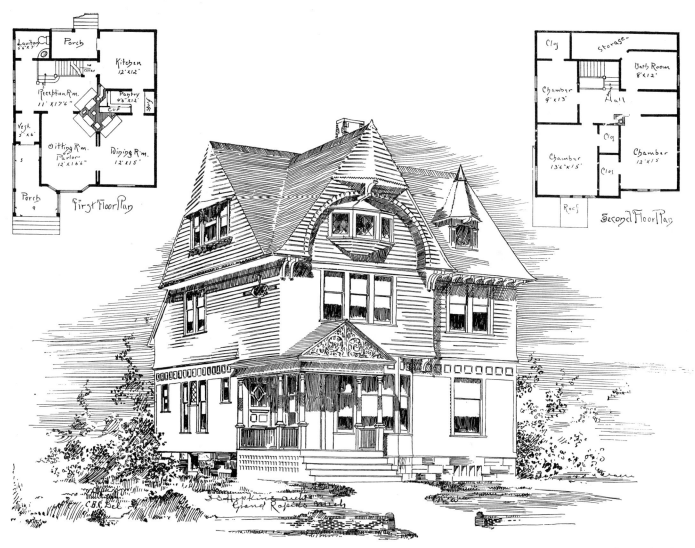

DESIGN NO. 113.

D. S. HOPKINS, Architect,

DESIGN NO. 113.

FRAME two story and attic dwelling. Size, 31 feet 6 inches by 40 feet over all. This is an economical stylish house nearly square, and only one chimney. Height of stories: First, 10 feet; second, 9 feet 6 inches. Cellar under entire house 7 feet deep. Stone foundation to cellar bottom. First story clapboarded and paneled. Second story and gables shingles. Shingle roof.

First story contains vestibule, 5x6 feet; reception hall, 11x17 feet 6 inches, with stair case and fire-place; parlor, with bay and fire-place, 12x16 feet 6 inches; dining room, with fire-place, 12x15 feet; kitchen, 12x12 feet; pantry, 4 feet 6 inches by 12 feet; lavatory off from stair hall, 5 feet 6 inches by 7 feet; kitchen porch, 6x10 feet; front porch, 6x15 feet.

Second story contains front chamber, 13x15 feet; chamber, 12x15 feet; chamber, 9x13 feet; bath room or chamber, 8x12 feet, with large closets to all chambers. Attic stairs can be run up over the other stairs if desired.

MODIFICATIONS: Principal rooms and hall, hardwood finish. Another room can be added to rear and present kitchen and pantry removed into same, and dining room put in place of present kitchen and pantry and sitting room made of dining room. Estimate cost as here shown, pine finish, no plumbing, mantels, grates or heating, $1,800 to $2,300.

See price list for cost of full plans, page vi.

The lowest estimate of cost is in accordance with price list of material and labor as given on page v, and by comparing with your local prices you can ascertain the cost of any of these buildings in your vicinity.

For changing shingles to clapboards on exterior of any design or reversing of plans, no extra charge will be made

D.S. Hopkins Arch't. ⊕⊕⊕⊕⊕⊕ Grand Rapids Mich.

DESIGN NO. 26.

D. S. HOPKINS, Architect.

PRINCIPAL FLOOR PLAN

DESIGN NO. 26.

FRAME one story and high attic. Size, 29x48 feet over all. Height of story, from 10 to 11 feet. Cellar under rear part of house 7 feet deep. Stone foundation to cellar bottom, around cellar. Sides clapboarded. Shingle roof.

First story contains hall, 4 feet 6 inches by 14 feet; parlor, 13x16 feet (with fire place); dining room, 13x1 feet, with fire-place; front chamber, 10 by 11 feet 6 inches; side chamber, 11x11 feet; child's room or dressing room, 8x8 feet; bath room, 5 feet 6 inches by 7 feet 6 inches; kitchen, 12x13 feet; pantry, 4x10 feet. With pine finish throughout and plumbing. No mantels, grates or heating.

MODIFICATIONS: Cellar under entire house. Design can be enlarged. Front chamber can be used as parlor, and parlor as sitting room. Bath room can be entered from dressing room and closed from dining room if preferred. There can be two fair sized rooms finished off in attic if desired.

Estimate cost as here shown, $1,500 to $2,000.

See price list for cost of full plans, page vi.

The lowest estimate of cost is in accordance with price list of material and labor as given on page v, and by comparing with your local prices, you can ascertain the cost of any of these buildings in your vicinity.

For changing shingles to clapboards on exterior of any design or reversing of plans, no extra charge will be made.

First Floor Plan

Second Floor Plan.

HOUSES AND COTTAGES.　　　**DESIGN NO. 125.**　　　*D. S. HOPKINS, Architect.*

DESIGN NO. 125.

FRAME two-story cottage. Size, 31x34 feet over all. Rather nice arrangement of interior; cozy and compact. Height of stories: First, 9 feet; second 8 feet 6 inches. Stone foundation. Cellar under kitchen, hall and reception hall. Stone to cellar bottom 7 feet deep. First story sides clapboarded; second story sides and gables shingles and shingle roof.

First story contains reception hall, 10x12 feet; parlor or sitting room, 13 feet 6 inches by 14 feet (with fire place); dining room, 13x15 feet (with fire place); stair hall, 7x11 feet; hat and coat closet, etc.; kitchen, 11 feet 6 inches by 12 feet; pantry, 5 feet 6 inches by 6 feet, and kitchen closet; front porch.

Second story contains bay chamber, 13 feet 6 inches by 14 feet (with fire place); other front chamber, 9x12 feet with balcony in front 5x12 feet, and chamber back 11x11 feet 6 inches; one on other side 11 feet 6 inches by 13 feet 6 inches; bath room, 4 feet 6 inches by 7 feet 6 inches and closets to all chambers.

MODIFICATIONS: Porch can extend across entire front if desired. Rooms can be generally enlarged if required. Stories can be made higher. Second story can be enclosed with clapboarding instead of shingles.

Estimate cost as here shown with hard wood finish in principal rooms and hall first floor, balance pine finish no plumbing, mantels, grates or heating, $2,000 to $2,500.

See price list for cost of full plans, page vi.

The lowest estimate of cost is in accordance with price list of material and labor as given on page v, and by comparing with your local prices, you can ascertain the cost of any of these buildings in your vicinity.

For changing shingles to clapboards on exterior of any design or reversing of plans, no extra charge will be made.

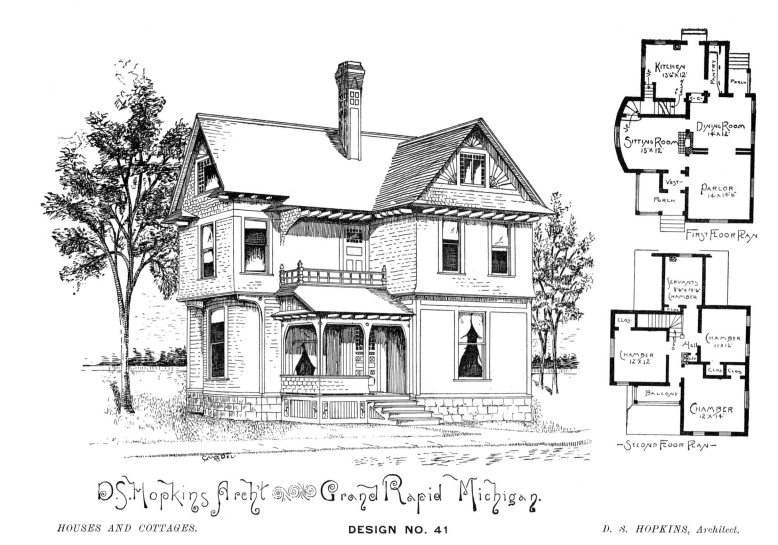

D.S. Hopkins Arch't Grand Rapid Michigan.

DESIGN NO. 41   *D. S. HOPKINS, Architect.*

DESIGN NO. 41.

FRAME two-story cottage. A very prepossessing exterior and pleasant interior. Size, 30x39 feet over all. Height of stories: First, 10 feet; second 9 feet 6 inches. Cellar under whole house. Stone foundation to bottom of cellar, 7 feet deep. First story clapboarded, second story shingles. Gables shingled and battens. Shingle roof.

First story contains vestibule, 3 feet 6 inches by 5 feet; parlor, 14x14 feet 6 inches; sitting room, 12x15 feet (with fire place); dining room, 12x14 feet; kitchen, 12x13 feet 6 inches; pantry, 4 feet 6 inches by 10 feet 6 inches. Stairs back and front. Front and rear porch.

Second floor contains front chamber, 12x14 feet; left side chamber, 12x12 feet; right side chamber, 11x12 feet; servant's room, 8 feet 6 inches by 10 feet 6 inches. Closets to all chambers. Balcony over porch. Pine finish. No mantel or grate.

MODIFICATIONS: Front porch could be enlarged and another one put over kitchen door. Rear part could be carried up same as main part and have chamber and bath room in same. House could be generally enlarged.

Estimate cost as here shown, $1,500 to $1,800.

See price list for cost of full plans, page vi.

The lowest estimate of cost is in accordance with price list of material and labor as given on page v, and by comparing with your local prices you can ascertain the cost of any of these buildings in your vicinity.

For changing shingles to clapboards on exterior of any design or reversing of plans, no extra charge will be made.

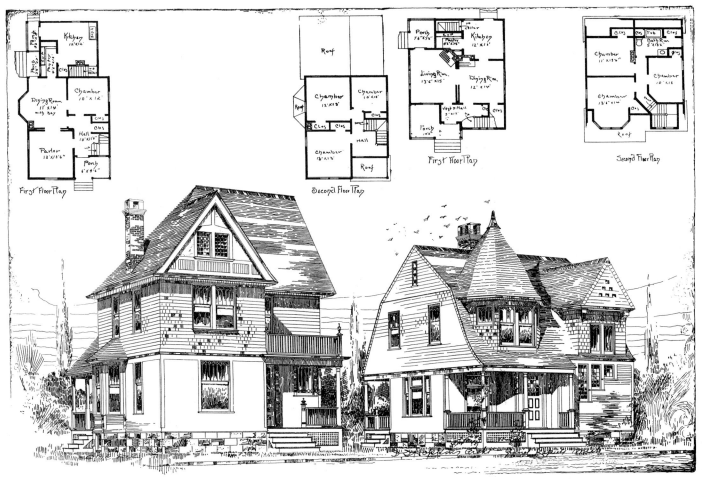

HOUSES AND COTTAGES.   **DESIGNS NOS. 133 AND 156.**   *D. S. HOPKINS, Architect.*

DESIGN NO. 133.

FRAME two-story cottage. A clever arrangement for a cheap house. Size 27x45 feet over all. Height of stories: first, 9 feet 2 inches; second, 8 feet 4 inches. Stone foundation. Cement bank shelf cellar under whole house back of parlor and hall 7 feet deep. First story sides clapboarded; second story sides shingles. Gables paneled. Shingle roof.

First story contains entrance and stair hall 10x11 feet 6 inches; parlor, 13x13 feet 6 inches; dining room, 11x14 feet, without bay; chamber, 10x12 feet; kitchen, 12x12 feet; pantry, 4 feet 6 inches by 10 feet. Rear, side and front porch.

Second floor contains front chamber 13x13 feet; one back, 12x13 feet; one 10x10 feet, and closets to each.

MODIFICATIONS: Cellar under whole house—stone to bottom. Rear wing carried up another half story and chamber and bath room put in over kitchen and rear stairs.

Estimate cost as here shown, pine finish, $1,400 to $1,800.

See price list for cost of full plans, page vi.

DESIGN NO. 156.

FRAME two-story cottage. Size 29x34 feet over all. Height of stories: first, 9 feet; second, 8 feet. Stone or brick foundation, and cement bank cellar under whole house 6 feet 6 inches deep. First story sides clapboarded; second story and gables shingled. Shingle roof.

First story contains vestibule and stair hall 5x12 feet; parlor, 13 feet 6 inches by 15 feet, with fire-place; dining room, 12x14 feet, with closet and fire-place; kitchen, 11x12 feet; pantry, 4 feet 6 inches by 7 feet 6 inches. Large rear and front porches.

Second story contains front chamber 13 feet 6 inches by 14 feet, and one 10x13 feet; rear side chamber, 11x13 feet 6 inches, and closets; bath room, 5x10 feet with closet.

MODIFICATIONS: Cellar under whole house, stone to bottom. More room can be added on back if desired.

Estimate cost as here shown, pine finish, no plumbing, mantels or grates, $1,200 to $1,500. Add for plumbing $175. Hardwood in two rooms and hall, add $50.

See price list for cost of full plans, page vi.

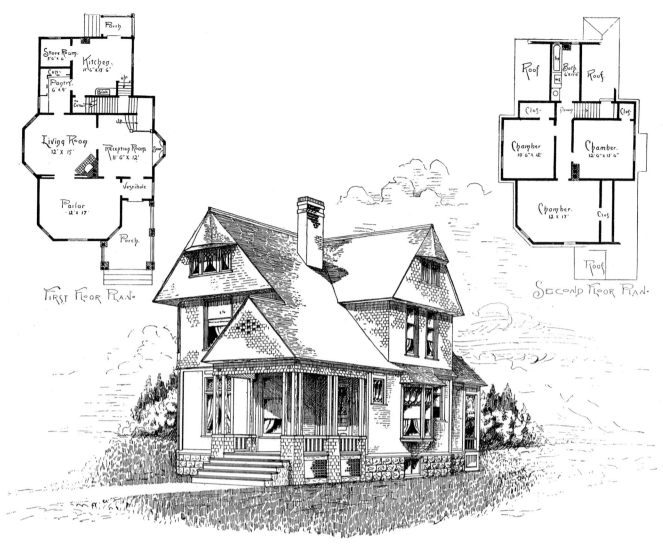

First Floor Plan.

Second Floor Plan.

DESIGN NO. 42.

D. S. HOPKINS, Architect.

DESIGN NO. 42.

TWO-STORY frame cottage. Size 28x48 feet, including front porch 8x10 feet. Height of stories: first, 9 feet; second, 8 feet 6 inches. Stone foundation and cellar under whole house 7 feet deep. First story sides clapboarded; second story and gables shingled. Shingle roof.

First story contains vestibule 4x6 feet 6 inches; reception hall, 11 feet 6 inches by 12 feet; parlor, 12x17 feet; living room, 12x15 feet, with fire-place; pantry, 6x8 feet; kitchen, 11 feet 6 inches by 13 feet 6 inches; store room, 5 feet 6 inches by 6 feet. Front and back combination stairs.

Second story contains three chambers and bath room, closets, etc. All pine finish. No plumbing, mantels or grates.

MODIFICATIONS: The rear part of this house can be changed so as to contain dining room, pantry and kitchen, and dining room used as sitting room. The same can be carried up one and a half stories, and chamber and bath room made of same.

Estimate cost as here shown, $1,800 to $2,200.

See price list for cost of full plans, page vi.

The lowest estimate of cost is in accordance with price list of material and labor as given on page v, and by comparing with your local prices, you can ascertain the cost of any of these buildings in your vicinity.

For changing shingles to clapboards on exterior of any design or reversing of plans, no extra charge will be made,

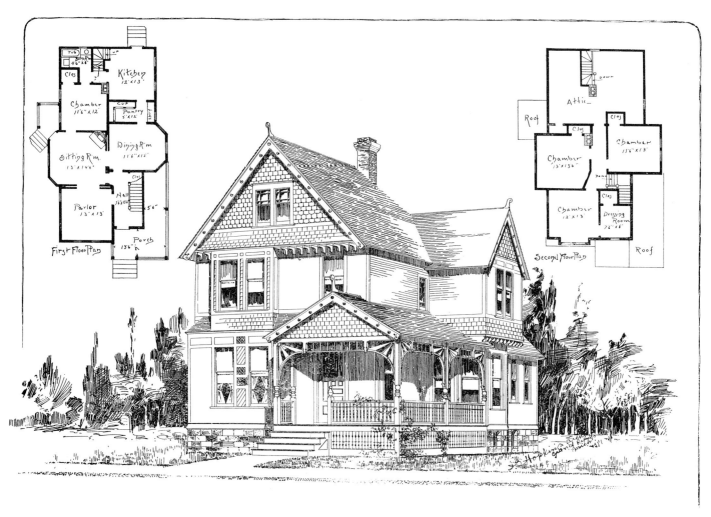

DESIGN NO. 145.

DESIGN NO. 145.

FRAME two-story cottage. Size 34x54 feet over all. Height of stories: first, 9 feet 6 inches: second, 8 feet. Stone foundation and cellar under sitting room and dining room and all back 7 feet deep. First and second story sides clapboarded, except a shingle belt over first story windows. Gables shingled and shingle roof.

First story contains entrance and stair hall 7 feet 6 inches by 13 feet 6 inches; parlor, 13x13 feet; sitting room, 13x14 feet 6 inches, with fire-place; dining room, 11 feet 6 inches by 15 feet; chamber, 11 feet 6 inches by 12 feet, with closet; kitchen, 11x13 feet; pantry, 5x12 feet; bath room, 5x8 feet. Front and rear stairs. Side entrance and large front porches.

Second story contains front bay chamber 12x13 feet, with dressing room adjoining, 7 feet 6 inches by 8 feet, and closet; side chamber, 13x13 feet; and one 11 feet 6 inches by 13 feet, with closets and unfinished storage room over wing.

MODIFICATIONS: Cellar under entire house. Whole house can be enlarged. Fire-place in chamber, second floor. Rear second floor can be finished so as to get another good room.

Estimate cost as here shown, pine finish, no plumbing, mantels, grates or heating, $1,800 to $2,300. Four rooms and hall finished in hard wood, add $80 over pine finish. Plumbing, $175.

See price list for cost of full plans, page vi.

The lowest estimate of cost is in accordance with price list of material and labor as given on page v, and by comparing with your local prices, you can ascertain the cost of any of these buildings in your vicinity.

For changing shingles to clapboards on exterior of any design or reversing of plans, no extra charge will be made.

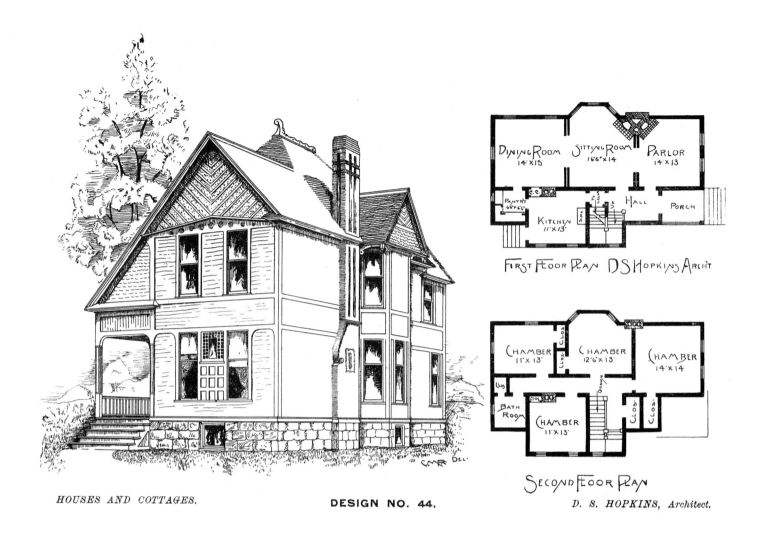

DINING ROOM 14×15 SITTING ROOM 16'6"×14 PARLOR 14×13

PANTRY 6'6"×6' C C HALL PORCH

KITCHEN 11'×13'

FIRST FLOOR PLAN DS HOPKINS ARCHT

CHAMBER 11'×13' CLOS CLOS CHAMBER 12'6"×13' CHAMBER 14'×14

CLOS CLOS CLOS

BATH ROOM CHAMBER 11'×13' CLOS CLOS

SECOND FLOOR PLAN

HOUSES AND COTTAGES. **DESIGN NO. 44.** *D. S. HOPKINS, Architect.*

DESIGN NO. 44.

FRAME two-story cottage. A small pleasant arrangement for a medium-size family. Size 29x44 feet over all. Height of stories: First 9 feet; second, 8 feet 6 inches. Cellar under entire house, 7 feet deep. Stone foundation to cellar bottom. First and second stories clapboarded; gables shingled and rough cast. Shingle roofs.

First story contains hall 6 feet 6 inches by 10 feet; parlor 13x14 feet (with fire place); dining room, 14x15 feet; sitting room, 14x16 feet 6 inches (with fire place); kitchen, 11x13 feet; pantry, 6 feet 6 inches by 6 feet 6 inches. Front stairs.

Second floor contains front chamber, 14x14 feet; side bay chamber, 12 feet 6 inches by 13 feet; opposite side chamber, 11x13 feet; rear chamber 11x13 feet; bath room 6 feet 6 inches by 7 feet. No attic stairs.

MODIFICATIONS: House can be generally enlarged. More porch can be provided in front if desired. Fire places can be placed in two chambers. Second story rear stairs could be arranged for.

Estimate cost as here shown, $1,800 to $2,500.

See price list for cost of full plans, page vi.

The lowest estimate of cost is in accordance with price list of material and labor as given on page v, and by comparing with your local prices you can ascertain the cost of any of these buildings in your vicinity.

For changing shingles to clapboards on exterior of any design or reversing of plans, no extra charge will be made

First Floor Plan

Second Floor Plan

HOUSES AND COTTAGES.   DESIGN NO. 146.   D. S. HOPKINS, Architect.

DESIGN NO. 146.

FRAME two story double tenement dwelling of moderate cost. Size, 35x42 feet over all. Height of stories: First, 9 feet 6 inches; second, 8 feet. Stone or brick foundation, and full stone cellar under dining rooms and kitchens. First story sides clapboarded. Second story and gables shingled. Shingle roof.

First story contains entrance hall with stairs from same 4x12 feet; sitting room, 12x14 feet; dining room, 11x13 feet; kitchen, 10x11 feet; pantry, 4 feet 6 inches by 10 feet; to cellar from kitchen; front porch.

Second floor contains three chambers on a side, one 12x14 feet; one 10x11 feet; and one 9x10 feet, and closets, with a balcony from one front room.

MODIFICATIONS: Fire place could be put in sitting room and dining room, also up stairs in two chambers on each side. Rooms could be enlarged and another one built back if desired.

Estimate cost as here shown, pine finish, $1,600 to $2,000.

See price list for cost of full plans, page vi.

The lowest estimate of cost is in accordance with price list of materal and labor as given on page v, and by comparing with your local prices, you can ascertain the cost of any of these buildings in your vicinity.

For changing shingles to clapboards on exterior of any design or reversing of plans, no extra charge will be made.

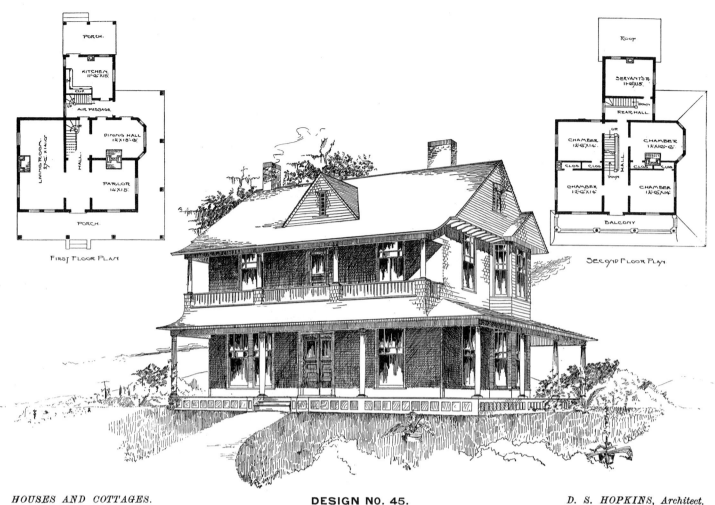

FIRST FLOOR PLAN

HOUSES AND COTTAGES.   DESIGN NO. 45.   D. S. HOPKINS, Architect.

DESIGN NO. 45.

FRAME two-story dwelling. Size, 45x65 feet, including front porch 8 feet wide and rear stove or laundry porch 10 feet wide. Height of stories: First, 11 feet; second, 10 feet. Stone and pier foundation. No cellar. First story sides clapboarded; second story and gables shingled. Shingle roof. This is a resort or southern style plan dwelling.

First story contains hall, 8x27 feet with stairs; parlor, 14x15 feet (with fire place); living room, 14x27 feet (with fire place); dining room, 12x16 feet 6 inches (with fire place); air passages between main part and kitchen 5 feet wide and rear stairs; kitchen, 12x15 feet; pantry, cupboards, etc.; also bath room, 5x8 feet.

Second floor contains large hall and balcony entire width of house, with four good-sized chambers and closets in main part, with servant's room over kitchen. Pine finish. No plumbing, mantels or grates.

MODIFICATIONS: Three more grates could be placed in second story chambers. Size of house could be changed. Bath room could be arranged for off from rear hall, second story, if desired.

Estimate cost as here shown, $2,000 to $2,500.

See price list for cost of full plans, page vi.

The lowest estimate of cost is in accordance with price list of material and labor as given on page v, and by comparing with your local prices, you can ascertain the cost of any of these buildings in your vicinity.

For changing shingles to clapboards on exterior of any design or reversing of plans, no extra charge will be made.

First Floor Plan

Second Floor Plan

HOUSES AND COTTAGES.   DESIGN NO. 147.   D. S. HOPKINS, Architect.

DESIGN NO. 147.

FRAME two-story cottage. Size, 30x44 feet over all. Height of stories: First, 9 feet 6 inches; second, 8 feet. Stone or brick foundation. Cement bank cellar under entire house 7 feet deep. First story sides clapboarded; second story sides shingles or clapboarding. Gables and roof shingles.

First story contains entrance and stair hall 8x17 feet with nook and fire place in front end. Sitting room, 12x15 feet (with fire place); dining room, 12x15 feet (with fire place); kitchen, 11x13 feet 6 inches (with closet and to cellar from same); combination stairs; pantry, 4 feet 6 inches by 9 feet 6 inches; rear and large front porch.

Second floor contains two front chambers, one 10 feet 6 inches by 13 feet 6 inches; one 12x14 feet 6 inches; one rear chamber, 12x12 feet; one 10x10 feet 6 inches; bath room, 5 feet 6 inches by 7 feet, and plenty of closets.

MODIFICATIONS: Stoned up cellar under whole house. Fire place in second story chambers. Another dining room could be built on back and rooms changed around so as to have a parlor.

Estimate cost as here shown, pine finish, no plumbing, mantels, grates or heating, $1,600 to $2,000.

See price list for cost of full plans, page vi.

The lowest estimate of cost is in accordance with price list of material and labor as given on page v, and by comparing with your local prices you can ascertain the cost of any of these buildings in your vicinity.

For changing shingles to clapboards on exterior of any design or reversing of plans, no extra charge will be made.

HOUSES AND COTTAGES.   **DESIGN NO. 46.**   *D. S. HOPKINS, Architect.*

DESIGN NO. 46.

FRAME two-story dwelling. A study for economy of room, convenience, etc., at small expense. Size 28x40 feet over all. Height of stories: first, 9 feet 6 inches; second, 8 feet. Cellar under entire house 7 feet deep. Stone foundation. Sides are clapboarded; gables shingled, shingle roof.

First story contains vestibule 4x6 feet; sitting hall, 13 feet 6 inches by 13 feet 6 inches, with fire-place; stair hall back of same; parlor, 13x15 feet, with fire-place; dining room, 12x15 feet, with fire-place; kitchen, 11 feet 6 inches by 12 feet; pantry, 6 feet 6 inches by 7 feet 6 inches. Front and rear side porches.

Second floor contains front chamber 12x13 feet; side front chamber, 10x13 feet; chamber back of stairs, 9x12 feet; and chamber 13x13 feet, with bath room 7 feet 6 inches by 9 feet, and attic stairs. Closets to all principal chambers. Main stairs are so arranged as to answer for both front and rear admirably. All pine finish.

MODIFICATIONS: Front porch can be enlarged, projecting out further from house. More room can be provided by building on another room on back of present kitchen and pantry, and use present kitchen as dining room. Provide rear stairs at same time and go to cellar under same, or some of these fire-places can be left out if desired and house cheapened some.

Estimate cost as here shown, $1,800 to $2,400.

See price list for cost of full plans, page vi.

First Floor Plan

Kitchen
11'x13'

Dining Room
11'x15'6"

Sitting Hall
12x15

Porch
4'x6'

Porch

Second Floor Plan

Bath Rm 4'6"x11'

Chamber
10'x9'

Chamber
13'x14'6"

Chamber
9'6"x15'

Roof

Roof

DESIGN NO. 148.

FRAME two-story and attic dwelling. A cozy little six-room home. Size 30x42 feet over all. Height of stories: first, 9 feet 6 inches; second, 8 feet. Stone foundation and cellar under entire house 7 feet deep. First and second stories clapboarded, gables paneled. Shingle roof.

First story contains vestibule 4 feet 6 inches by 4 feet 6 inches; sitting hall, with bay and fire-place, 12x15 feet; dining room, 11x15 feet 6 inches, with fire-place; kitchen, 11x13 feet; pantry, 4 feet 6 inches by 11 feet. Combination stairs. Side porch to kitchen and large front porch.

Second story contains front chamber, with bay, 9 feet 6 inches by 15 feet; chamber back, connecting with door (with fire-place) 13x16 feet, and rear chamber 10 feet 6 inches by 11 feet; bath room, 4 feet 6 inches by 7 feet, and plenty of closets.

MODIFICATIONS: Another room for dining room could be built back, with slight change of pantry, for dining room, and present dining room used as sitting room. Rooms could all be enlarged if desired. Exterior enclosure could be changed.

Estimate cost as here shown, with hardwood finish of two rooms first floor and pantry, no mantels, grates or heating, $1,700 to $2,200.

See price list for cost of full plans, page vi.

The lowest estimate of cost is in accordance with price list of material and labor as given on page v, and by comparing with your local prices you can ascertain the cost of any of these buildings in your vicinity.

For changing shingles to clapboards on exterior of any design, or reversing of plans, no extra charge will be made.

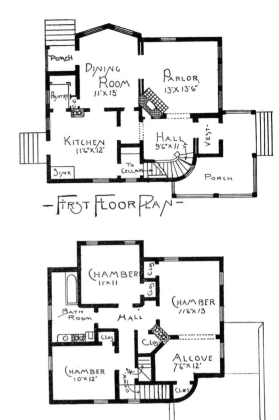

D·S·Hopkins·Arch't.
Grand Rapids. Mich.

F.M.B. Del.

HOUSES AND COTTAGES.   **DESIGN NO. 48.**   *D. S. HOPKINS, Architect.*

DESIGN NO. 48.

FRAME two-story cottage. This is rather a quaint little house exteriorly, and a very compact interior. Size 32x38 feet over all. This would make a very pretty exterior for certain localities. Height of stories: first, 9 feet; second, 8 feet 6 inches. Cellar under whole house. Stone foundation. First story clapboards; second shingled. Gable to turret shingled. Shingle roof.

First story contains vestibule 4x6 feet 6 inches; hall, 9 feet 6 inches by 11 feet; parlor, 13x13 feet 6 inches, with fire-place; dining room, 11x15 feet; kitchen, 11 feet 6 inches by 12 feet; pantry, 5x6 feet 6 inches. Large porch in front. Small porch at dining room entrance.

Second floor contains front chamber 11 feet 6 inches by 13 feet, and alcove adjoining 7 feet 6 inches by 12 feet; right side chamber, 11x11 feet; and chamber 10x12 feet, with bath room, 8x12 feet 6 inches. Closets to all chambers. All pine finish. No plumbing, mantels, grates or heating.

MODIFICATIONS: Exterior can be changed in front by raising the front lean-to to height of main, and bringing gables out to front. Turret remains same as now. Another room can be built on back of present kitchen and said kitchen used as dining room, and put in rear stairs also if desired. Pantry will work same as now, only change and close up some doors.

Estimate cost as here shown, $1,800 to $2,400.

See price list for cost of full plans, page vi.

The lowest estimate of cost is in accordance with price list of material and labor as given on page v, and by comparing with your local prices, you can ascertain the cost of any of these buildings in your vicinity.

For changing shingles to clapboards on exterior of any design or reversing of plans, no extra charge will be made.

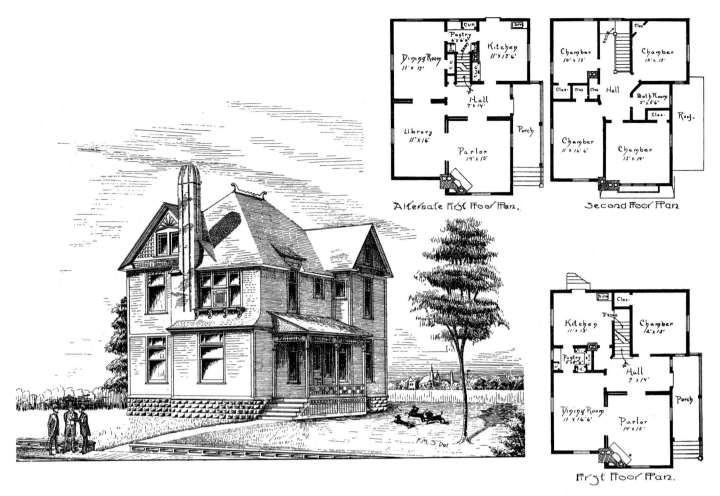

DESIGN NO. 50.

DESIGN NO. 50.

FRAME two-story dwelling. This house is built in the most economical form, nearly square, and so arranged to give best rooms in front, and is shown in two ways on floor plans, with and without chamber on first floor. Size 33x38 feet over all. Height of stories: first, 10 feet; second, 9 feet 6 inches. Cellar under whole house 7 feet deep. Stone foundation to cellar bottom. First story clapboarded; second story clapboarded and shingled. Gables shingled and paneled. Shingle roof.

First story contains hall 7x14 feet; parlor, 14x15 feet, with fire-place; dining room, 11x16 feet 6 inches; pantry, 5x7 feet 6 inches; kitchen, 11x13 feet; closets, stairs and front side porch.

Second story contains front main chamber 13x14 feet; front side chamber 11x16 feet 6 inches; rear side chamber, 12x13 feet; servant's chamber, 10x13 feet; bath room 5x8 feet 6 inches; with closets for each chamber. All pine finish. No plumbing, mantels, grates or heating.

MODIFICATIONS: Front porch can be brought out to corner and across the front if desired. Rooms can be enlarged. Porch can be cut off in front of front door and enclosed and used as vestibule, and front door placed on porch fronting street, also door can be cut from kitchen to said vestibule if desired, also rear stairs provided for.

Estimate cost as here shown, $1,900 to $2,500.

See price list for cost of full plans, page vi.

The lowest estimate of cost is in accordance with price list of material and labor as given on page v, and by comparing with your local prices, you can ascertain the cost of any of these buildings in your vicinity.

For changing shingles to clapboards on exterior of any design or reversing of plans, no extra charge will be made.

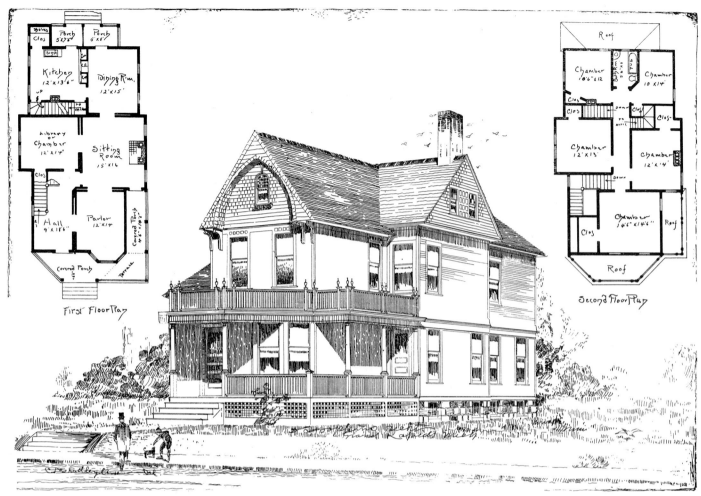

First Floor Plan

Second Floor Plan

HOUSES AND COTTAGES,   DESIGN NO. 154.   D. S. HOPKINS, Architect,

DESIGN NO. 154.

FRAME two story dwelling. Size, 31x60 feet over all. Height of stories: First, 10 feet; second, 9 feet 6 inches. Cellar under entire house. Stone foundation and cellar 7 feet deep. Sides clapboarded, gables shingles. Shingle roof.

First story contains hall, 9x18 feet 6 inches, with open stairs; parlor, 12x14 feet, with bay; sitting room, 15x16 feet, with fire-place; chamber or library, 12x14 feet, with closet; dining room, 12x15 feet; kitchen, 12x13 feet 6 inches; cupboards, china closet and kitchen closet; rear stairs and to cellar from kitchen; back and front porches.

Second story contains front chamber, 14 feet 6 inches by 14 feet 6 inches; chamber, 12x14 feet; chamber, 12x13 feet; two rear chambers, 10 feet 6 inches by 12 feet, and 10x14 feet; bath room, 5 feet 6 inches by 8 feet, with closets to all and attic stairs.

MODIFICATIONS: Porch in front could be roofed continuous if desired. Fire-place could be put in chamber over sitting room. Lavatory could be arranged for next to kitchen. Closets on rear porch. Contracted for and built as here shown, with four principal rooms and hall in hardwood finish, balance pine, hot air pipes for second floor, no plumbing, mantels, grates or heating, $2,375. Plumbing and gas pipes add $225.

See price list for cost of full plans, page vi.

The lowest estimate of cost is in accordance with price list of material and labor as given on page v, and by comparing with your local prices, you can ascertain the cost of any of these buildings in your vicinity.

For changing shingles to clapboards on exterior of any design or reversing of plans, no extra charge will be made.

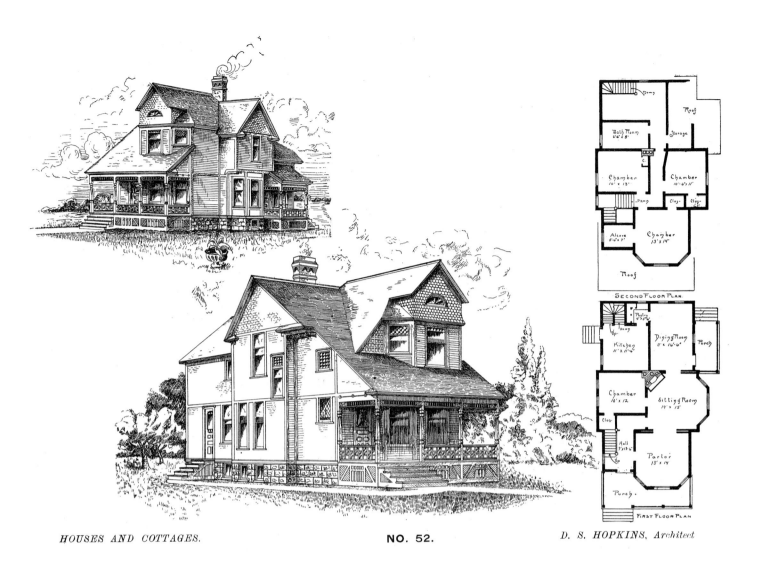

DESIGN NO. 52.

FRAME two story cottage. A style of house many want. A cheap house with chamber upon first floor. Size, 31x51 feet over all. Height of stories: First, 9 feet; second, 8 feet 6 inches. Square ceiling in main second story. Stone foundation, with cellar under kitchen, dining room and sitting room, 7 feet deep. Sides clapboarded, gables shingled. Shingle roof.

First story contains hall, 7x13 feet 6 inches; parlor, 13x14 feet; sitting room, 14x15 feet, with fire-place; chamber, 10x12 feet, with closet; dining room, 11x16 feet 6 inches; kitchen, 11x11 feet 6 inches; pantry, 5x5 feet 6 inches. Back and front stairs, front and side porches.

Second story contains front bay chamber, 13x14 feet, with alcove adjoining, 5 feet 6 inches by 7 feet; chamber back of stairs, 10x13 feet; chamber opposite, 10 feet 6 inches by 11 feet, and bath room, 6 feet 6 inches by 8 feet, with storage room in abundance. Pine finish. No plumbing, mantels, grate or heating.

MODIFICATIONS: Some parties do not like this long roof down over porch. Same can be changed and the roof made in two parts and main cornice running around and joining the front, same as on the other side as per upper perspective. Fire-place can be arranged for in dining room and chamber if desired. Wing second story can be divided up in one or two more chambers by raising the low side to balance the other. Estimate cost as here shown, $1,800 to $2,200.

See price list for cost of full plans, page vi.

The lowest estimate of cost is in accordance with price list of material and labor as given on page v, and by comparing with your local prices you can ascertain the cost of any of these buildings in your vicinity.

For changing shingles to clapboards on exterior of any design or reversing of plans, no extra charge will be made.

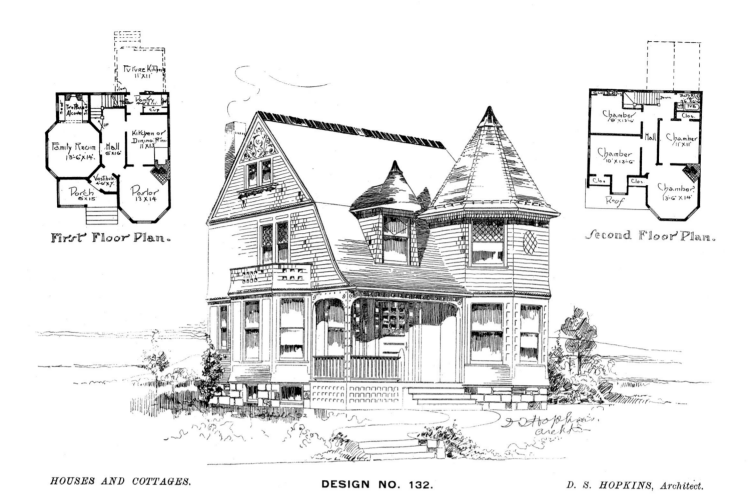

First Floor Plan.

Second Floor Plan.

HOUSES AND COTTAGES.   **DESIGN NO. 132.**   *D. S. HOPKINS, Architect.*

DESIGN NO. 132.

FRAME two story cottage. Size, 33x34 feet. A very compact and cozy cottage. Most room for the money is the motto here. Height of stories: First, 9 feet 6 inches; second, 8 feet; stone foundation and cellar under family room, hall and alcove. Stone cellar to bottom. First story sides clapboarded. Second story sides shingled; gables shingles and scrolls. Shingle roof.

First story contains vestibule, 4 feet 6 inches by 7 feet; family room, 13 feet 6 inches by 14 feet, with alcove 7 by 8 feet, and fire-place in same; hall, 6x16 feet, with open stairs in back; dining room or parlor, 13x14 feet, with fire-place; dining room or kitchen, 11x13 feet; pantry, 4 feet 6 inches by 11 feet; future kitchen; 11x11 feet; to cellar from pantry.

Second story contains front family chamber, 13 feet 6 inches by 14 feet, with fire-place; children's room back, 11x11 feet; two chambers on other side of hall, one 10x13 feet 6 inches; one 9x13 feet 6 inches; bath room, 4 feet 6 feet and closets to all chambers.

MODIFICATIONS: Kitchen can be built on back as kitchen and present kitchen used as dining room, and front room as parlor where more room is desired. Rooms can be enlarged if required.

Estimate cost as here shown without future kitchen, with hardwood finish for first floor, principal rooms and hall; also plumbing, no mantels, grates or heating, $2,000 to $2,500. If no plumbing, deduct $200. If no hardwood, deduct $100.

See price list for cost of full plans, page vi.

The lowest estimate of cost is in accordance with price list of material and labor as given on page v. and by comparing with your local prices you can ascertain the cost of any of these buildings in your vicinity.

For changing shingles to clapboards on exterior of any design or reversing of plans, no extra charge will be made.

DESIGN NO. 75.

D. S. HOPKINS, Architect.

DESIGN NO. 75.

FRAME two story dwelling. Size, 30x68 feet, including an 8-foot porch in front and 10-foot porch in rear. Height of stories: First, 11 feet 6 inches by 10 feet 6 inches. No cellar. Brick foundation and piers. First story sides clapboarded, second story and gables shingles; Shingle roof. This is a southern style of house. The first floor is so arranged as to throw all main part rooms and hall together if desired.

First story contains hall, 10x19 feet, with stair case; living room, 15x20 feet, with fire-place; dining room, 12x18 feet, with fire-place; 5-foot open space between dining room and kitchen; kitchen 13x15 feet, with store pantry, cupboards, etc. Back of the kitchen is a 10 foot porch, with back stairs from same. This porch is intended to set stove on for laundry use, etc.

Second floor contains large hall, a bath room or another chamber could be made, if desired, off from it; two good-sized chambers, and two rear rooms, closets, etc. Two fire-places could be arranged on second floor directly over those below, if desired, by making slight changes in closets. Pine finish.

MODIFICATIONS: Size of rooms and size of house changed. Side of main porch could be widened out to line of hall projection. Two fire-places could be provided for in chambers. Second story: Bath room could be arranged for upon second story if desired, by reducing size of one rear chamber and loss of one closet. Estimate cost is from $1,800 to $2,300.

See price list for cost of full plans, page vi.

The lowest estimate of cost is in accordance with price list of material and labor as given on page v, and by comparing with your local prices, you can ascertain the cost of any of these buildings in your vicinity.

For changing shingles to clapboards on exterior of any design or reversing of plans, no extra charge will be made.

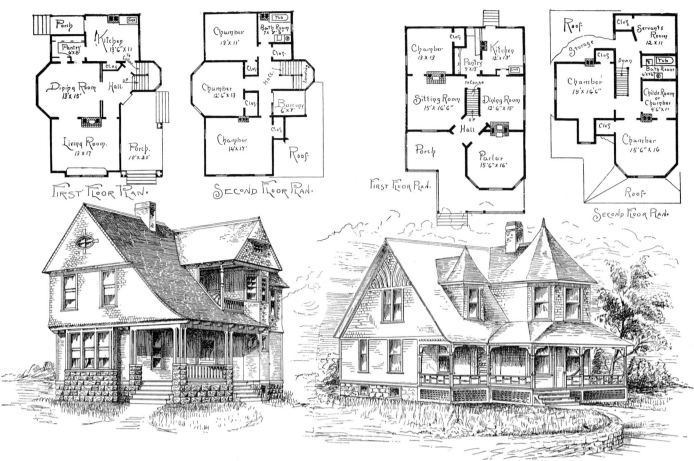

HOUSES AND COTTAGES.   DESIGNS NOS. 36 AND 37.   D. S. HOPKINS, Architect.

DESIGN NO. 36.

FRAME two-story cottage. Size 32x40 feet; exterior size including front porch, 10x19 feet. Height of stories, first, 9 feet; second, 8 feet 6 inches. Stone foundation and cellar under whole house. This design is intended for those who want a neat, common-sense dwelling where the whole house will be used (no shut up parlors only to be used for weddings and funerals) but live in front of the house themselves. All rooms of good size and really contains ⌐all the luxuries there are in an expensive house.

First story has some extra rock faced stone work in front and about the porch, balance clapboarding. Second story and gables shingled; shingle roof. First story painted three coats, second story and gables stained.

First story contains stair hall, 8x11 feet; living room, 13x17 feet, (with fire place); dining room, 13x15 feet; kitchen 11x13 feet 6 inches; pantry 6x8 feet, and rear porch.

Second story contains three good sized chambers, closets and bath room, balcony, etc. All pine finish. No mantels, grates, plumbing or heating.

MODIFICATIONS: Stone work above foundation can be substituted with wood. Fire place in dining room. Rear stairs could be provided and another kitchen could be built on back and present kitchen used as dining room, and dining room as sitting room. Pantry could be changed in that event.

Estimate cost is $1,800 to $2,300.

See price list for cost of full plans, page vi.

DESIGN NO. 37.

FRAME one and one-half story cottage. Size 34x52 feet, including front porch, 6 feet wide. Height of stories: First, 9 feet 6 inches; second, 9 feet. Stone foundation. Cellar under sitting room and dining room, 7 feet deep. First story clapboarded; second story shingled. Shingle roof.

First story contains hall, 6x8 feet; parlor, 15 feet 6 inches by 16 feet (with fire place); sitting room 15x16 feet 6 inches (with fire place); dining room, 12 feet 6 inches by 15 feet (with fire place; chamber, 13x13 feet; kitchen, 12x13 feet, and pantry, 7x13 feet. Very large front porch. Front stairs.

Second story contains four chambers; closets and bath room. All pine finish. No plumbing, mantels, grates or heating.

MODIFICATIONS: Cellar under whole house. Bath room could be arranged off from chamber first floor by building on back. Second story could be full height throughout and another chamber provided in place of storage room.

Estimate cost as here shown, $1,800 to $2,100.

See price list for cost of full plans, page vi.

32

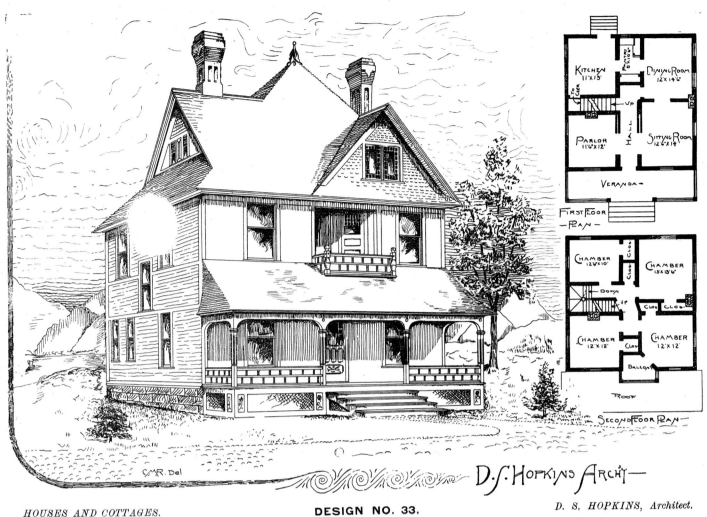

DESIGN NO. 33.

FRAME two-story cottage. This is a square house, the cheapest style of house to build. Size 30x37 feet, including front porch. Height of stories: first, 10 feet; second, 9 feet 6 inches. Cement bank cellar under entire house 6 feet 6 inches deep. Stone foundation. Sides clapboarded, gables shingled, shingle roof.

First story contains hall 4x18 feet; parlor, 11 feet 6 inches by 12 feet; sitting room, 12 feet 6 inches by 14 feet; dining room, 12x14 feet 6 inches; kitchen, 11x13 feet; pantry, 5x10 feet 6 inches. Large veranda across the front.

Second floor contains two front chambers 12x12 feet; rear chamber, 13x13 feet 6 inches; one chamber, 10x12 feet 6 inches, and five closets. Stairs to attic. Also a good, large balcony over front porch. Finished in pine.

MODIFICATIONS: Veranda can be widened out to 6 or 7 feet wide in front. Stoned up cellar under whole house. General enlargement if desired. Fire-place in sitting room, dining room and parlor if desired.

Estimated cost is from $1,600 to $2,000.

See price list for cost of full plans, page vi.

The lowest estimate of cost is in accordance with price list of material and labor as given on page v, and by comparing with your local prices, you can ascertain the cost of any of these buildings in your vicinity.

For changing shingles to clapboards on exterior of any design or reversing of plans, no extra charge will be made.

DESIGN NO. 32.

D. S. HOPKINS, Architect.

DESIGN NO. 32.

THIS is a pleasing arrangement of rooms, and has the accommodation of a more pretentious house. Size 27x49 feet. Frame house. Height of stories: first, 9 feet 6 inches; second, 8 feet. Cellar under kitchen, wood house and sitting room, 7 feet deep. Stone foundation.

First story contains hall 8x13 feet; parlor, 14x14 feet; sitting room, 12 feet 6 inches by 14 feet, with fireplace; dining room, 11 feet 6 inches by 14 feet; pantry, 5x12 feet; kitchen, 12x11 feet 6 inches, wood house 6x11 feet 6 inches.

Second story contains front chamber 14x14 feet; left chamber, 10x14 feet 6 inches, and right chamber 11x14 feet; rear chamber, 11 feet 6 inches by 12 feet, with store room 6x8 feet, and closets for all chambers. Pine finish. No plumbing, mantels, grates or heating. First and second floors clapboards. Gables paneled, shingled and scroll work.

MODIFICATIONS: Cellar under whole house. Wood house could be enlarged and made into a small chamber. Store room on second floor could be arranged for bath room.

Estimated cost as here shown, $1,500 to $1,800.

See price list for cost of full plans, page vi.

The lowest estimate of cost is in accordance with price list of material and labor as given on page v, and by comparing with your local prices, you can ascertain the cost of any of these buildings in your vicinity.

For changing shingles to clapboards on exterior of any design or reversing of plans, no extra charge will be made.

DESIGN NO. 31.

FRAME two-story cottage. Size 28x44 feet—nearly square. With every part of room economized it makes a very cheap, pleasant home. Height of stories: first, 10 feet; second, 9 feet 6 inches. Cellar under whole house 7 feet deep. Stone foundation to cellar bottom. Sides clapboarded; gables, fancy battens and panels. Shingle roof.

First story contains vestibule 4x6 feet, with closet; reception hall, 10x12 feet; parlor, 13 feet 6 inches by 16 feet 6 inches, with fire-place; dining room, 12x13 feet 6 inches; kitchen, 10x12 feet; pantry, 7x11 feet. Front and back stairs. Front and rear porches.

Second story contains front chamber 12x13 feet, and one 11 feet 6 inches by 17 feet 6 inches, and back of same chambers 10x10 feet and 10x11 feet; bath room, 7x7 feet 6 inches. Attic stairs, and closets to all chambers. All pine finish. No plumbing, mantels, grates or heating.

MODIFICATIONS: House can be enlarged by building another room on back of pantry for kitchen. Dining room side carried out in line with hall and partition between same and kitchen moved over in line with hall, and present kitchen, with a bay, would be library or sitting room. Rear stairs could be moved.

Estimate cost as here shown, $1,700 to $2,200.

See price list for cost of full plans, page vi.

·FIRST·FLOOR·PLAN·

·SECOND·FLOOR·PLAN·

HOUSES AND COTTAGES.

DESIGN NO. 21.

D. S. HOPKINS, Architect.

DESIGN NO. 21.

FRAME one and a half story cottage. Size 27x50 feet, including front porch 6 feet 8 inches wide by 27 feet long. This makes a compact, pretty house, and inexpensive. Height of stories: first, 9 feet; second, 8 feet. Stone foundation. Cement shelf bank cellar 7 feet deep. First story sides clapboarded; second story and gables shingled. Shingle roof.

First story contains reception hall 13x13 feet 6 inches; parlor, 12x14 feet; dining room, 14x14 feet 6 inches; kitchen, 11 feet 6 inches by 13 feet; pantry, 4x9 feet; chamber, 11x12 feet 6 inches; bath room, 5x9 feet, and closet; kitchen porch, 5x13 feet.

Second story contains four fair sized chambers and closets. All pine finish. No plumbing.

MODIFICATIONS: This house is supposed to be heated with furnace. Fire-place in living room. House can be enlarged if desired. Rear part can be carried up so as to get more chambers if desired. Stoned up cellar.

Estimate cost as here shown, $1,400 to $1,700.

See price list for cost of full plans, page vi.

The lowest estimate of cost is in accordance with price list of material and labor as given on page v, and by comparing with your local prices you can ascertain the cost of any of these buildings in your vicinity.
For changing shingles to clapboards on exterior of any design or reversing of plans, no extra charge will be made.

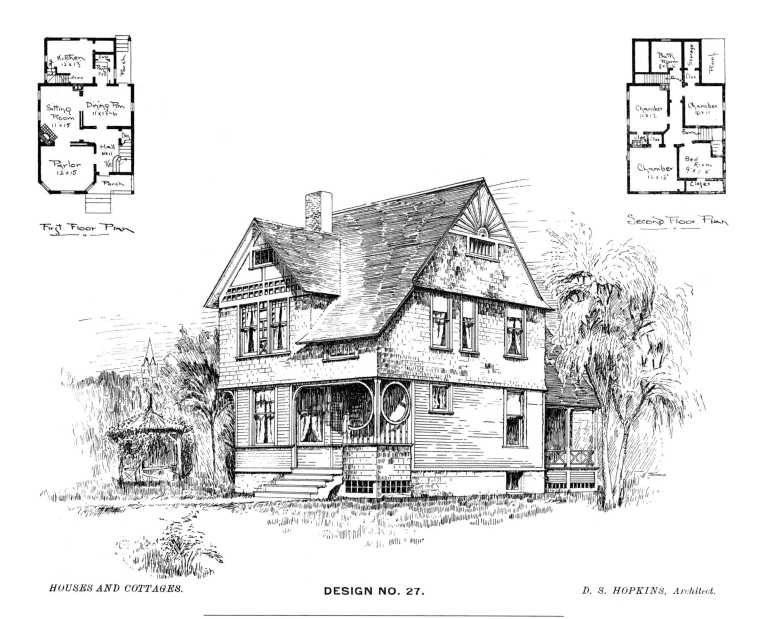

HOUSES AND COTTAGES.   **DESIGN NO. 27.**   *D. S. HOPKINS, Architect.*

DESIGN NO. 27.

FRAME two-story cottage. Size 26x41 feet. This is one of those cottages that many won't believe can be built for price given, because it is such a beauty, and at the same time has so much room and yet so compact. Height of stories: first, 9 feet 6 inches; second, 9 feet. Cellar under sitting room, dining room and kitchen, 7 feet deep. Stone foundation from cellar bottom. First story clapboarded; second story shingled. Gables paneled and shingled. Shingle roof.

First story contains hall 6x11 feet, with front stairs; parlor, 12x15 feet; sitting room, 11x15 feet, with fireplace; dining room, 11x13 feet 6 inches; kitchen, 12x13 feet; pantry, 5x8 feet; store closet, 5x4 feet. Back stairs out of kitchen, and down stairs under same. Porch on front and side.

Second story contains front chamber, 12x13 feet; front chamber, 8x9 feet; right side chamber, 11x12 feet; left side chamber, 10x11 feet; bath room, 8x8 feet 6 inches, with nice closets to each. Gas piping complete, and hot air pipes for second floor.

MODIFICATIONS: Fire-place in parlor can be provided. A bay can be put on sitting room or dining room. Rear part can be carried up so as to have another chamber at one side of bath room. More porch can be had by running same across the front.

Estimate cost as here shown, $1,500 to $1,800.

See price list for cost of full plans, page vi.

The lowest estimate of cost is in accordance with price list of material and labor as given on page v, and by comparing with your local prices you can ascertain the cost of any of these buildings in your vicinity.

For changing shingles to clapboards on exterior of any design, or reversing of plans, no extra charge will be made.

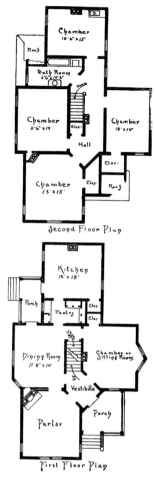

DESIGN NO. 30.

FRAME one and one-half story, or nearly full two-story house. A pleasant, home-like cottage. Stone foundation. Size 38x48 feet. Cellar under main part 7 feet deep. Height of stories: first, 9 feet; second, 8 feet 6 inches. Enclosure—clapboarding, ceiling, shingles and paneling. Shingle roof.

First story contains entrance vestibule and stair entrance 5x6 feet; parlor, 13x14 feet 6 inches, with fire-place; chamber or sitting room, 12x14 feet; dining room, 11 feet 6 inches by 14 feet; pantry, 5x9 feet 6 inches; kitchen, 12x13 feet. Closets, front and side porches.

Second story contains front chamber 13x15 feet; chamber back of same, 11 feet 6 inches by 14 feet; side chamber, 10x14 feet; bath room, 6 feet 6 inches by 10 feet 6 inches; servant's room, 10 feet 6 inches by 13 feet, with closets. All pine finish. No plumbing, mantels, grates or heating.

MODIFICATIONS: By taking about three feet off from side of chamber and moving chimney, an open stair case can be had, and said chamber can be enlarged by moving out the end two or three feet. This room would then make a pleasant dining room. Pantry would then want to be moved over back of same and present dining room would come in as a sitting room. Fire-place in parlor could be moved over against stairs in sitting room, and doors between same and parlor made larger if desired. A fire-place in chamber could be provided.

Estimate cost as here shown, $1,400 to $1,800.

See price list for cost of full plans, page vi.

·FIRST·FLOOR·PLAN·

·SECOND·FLOOR·PLAN·

HOUSES AND COTTAGES.   **DESIGN NO. 49.**   *D. S. HOPKINS, Architect.*

DESIGN NO. 49.

FRAME two-story dwelling. Size 36x44 feet, including bay at dining room, and front· porch 6 feet wide. Height of stories: first, 9 feet 6 inches; second, 9 feet. Stone foundation and cellar under whole house 7 feet deep. First and second story sides clapboarded. Gables shingled. Shingle roof.

First story contains vestibule 5x5 feet 6 inches; hall, 6x19 feet. Stairs can be made open or as shown. Parlor, 12 feet 6 inches by 14 feet; sitting room, 13x18 feet, with fire-place; dining room, 12x16 feet; pantry, 5 feet 6 inches by 12 feet; kitchen, 13x13 feet 6 inches, with closet, cupboards, entry, back stairs, etc.

Second floor contains five good sized chambers and closets to each, bath room, attic stairs, etc. All pine finish. No plumbing, mantels or grates.

MODIFICATIONS: Front stairs can be open if desired and wash bowl remain with portiere front, or be moved under stairs where closet now is by change of closet in front chamber, second story. Another fire-place can be provided. Front porch can be widened out and rear porch provided.

Estimate cost as here shown, $2,500 to $3,000.

See price list for cost of full plans, page vi.

The lowest estimate of cost is in accordance with price list of material and labor as given on page v, and by comparing with your local prices you can ascertain the cost of any of these buildings in your vicinity.

For changing shingles to clapboards on exterior of any design or reversing of plans, no extra charge will be made.

HOUSES AND COTTAGES.   **DESIGN NO. 51.**   *D. S. HOPKINS, Architect.*

DESIGN NO. 51.

FRAME one and a half story cottage. Size, 30x50 feet, not including side porch, which is 8x28 feet, with terrace in front 5x20 feet. This is a quaint picturesque design. The plan has many meritorious points, multum in parvo, for one. Height of stories: First, 9 feet; second, 8 feet 6 inches. Stone foundation and cellar under main part, 7 feet deep. Sides first story clapboarded, second story and gables shingled. Shingle roof.

First story contains vestibule, 4x7 feet; reception hall, 13x15 feet; parlor, 13x16 feet 6 inches, with fire-place; dining room, 12x16 feet; chamber, 11 feet 6 inches by 12 feet; bath room, 5x9 feet 6 inches; pantry, 5x12 feet; kitchen, 12 feet 6 inches by 14 feet; fuel room, kitchen closet and kitchen porch.

Second floor contains four medium sized chambers and closets. All pine finish. No mantels, grates or plumbing.

MODIFICATIONS: Vestibule can be omitted, and reception room can be used as stair or reception hall. Front stairs can be provided in same. Fire-place can be provided in front chamber, second floor. Rear second story can be carried up and another chamber or two can be provided. Estimate cost as here shown, $2,000 to $2,600.

See price list for cost of full plans, page vi.

The lowest estimate of cost is in accordance with price list of material and labor as given on page v, and by comparing with your local prices, you can ascertain the cost of any of these buildings in your vicinity.

For changing shingles to clapboards on exterior of any design or reversing of plans, no extra charge will be made.

DESIGN NO. 53.

DESIGN NO. 53.

FRAME two story cottage. Size, 37x70 feet, including rear porch 6 feet, and front porch 8 feet wide. Height of stories: First, 11 feet; second, 10 feet. No cellar. Set on posts or piers. Sides clapboarded, gables shingled. This is a resort or Southern style dwelling.

First story contains an 8 foot front porch on side and front with circular corners; parlor, 15x20 feet, with large fire-place; stair hall, 12 feet 6 inches by 15 feet, opening into dining room 15x15 feet (with large opening). The whole of this first floor opens up about the same as one room if desired. Back of this main part is an open passage 7 feet wide, containing rear stairs; pantry, 5x10 feet 6 inches; large closet and kitchen, 12x15 feet, in rear wing.

Second story contains three good sized chambers; hall and closets in main part with bath room and servant's room, hall, etc., in the rear part. Pine finish throughout. No plumbing.

MODIFICATIONS: Set on foundation with cellar. Take space occupied with open hall, pantry, closet, etc., and make a dining room of same, use a piece off from side kitchen porch for pantry extend up into dining room, so as to get door into pantry as well as from kitchen. These changes make a good all-the-year-around house. Other fire-places can be provided for if desired.

Estimate cost as here shown, $2,200 to $2,800.

See price list for cost of full plans, page vi.

The lowest estimate of cost is in accordance with price list of material and labor as given on page v, and by comparing with your local prices you can ascertain the cost of any of these buildings in your vicinity.

For changing shingles to clapboards on exterior of any design or reversing of plans, no extra charge will be made

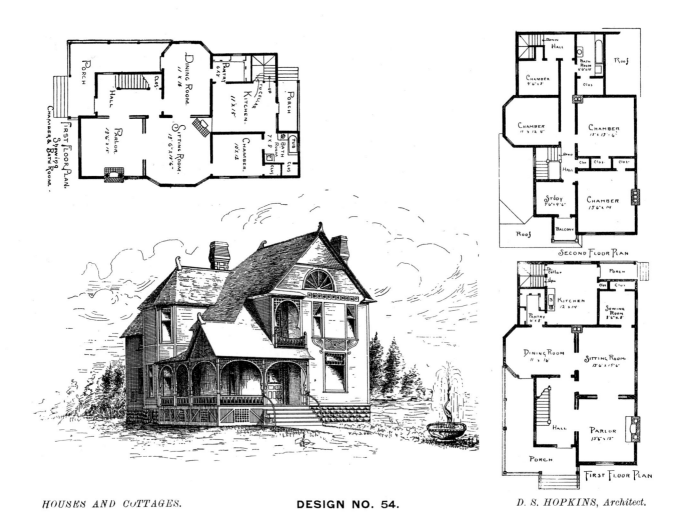

HOUSES AND COTTAGES. **DESIGN NO. 54.** D. S. HOPKINS, Architect.

DESIGN NO. 54.

FRAME two-story and attic dwelling.   Size 32x49 feet over all.   A pleasant cozy home for anyone.   This is designed in two heights, studding 18 feet 4 inches and 20 feet 4 inches (as shown in view); 18 feet 4 inch posts.   Stories, first, 9 feet; second, 8 feet 6 inches; 20 feet 4 inch posts.   Stories are, first, 10 feet; second, 9 feet 6 inches.   Cellar under entire house 7 feet deep, of stone, and stone foundation.   Sides clapboarded.   Gables shingled.   Shingle roof.

First story contains front stair hall 9x15 feet 6 inches; parlor, 13 feet 6 inches by 15 feet, with fire-place; sitting room, 13 feet 6 inches by 15 feet 6 inches; dining room, 11x16 feet.   The two last named rooms can have fire-places in each if desired in corners connecting with kitchen chimney.   Sewing room, 8 feet 6 inches by 8 feet; kitchen, 12x14 feet; pantry, 6x8 feet.   Back stairs.   Front and rear porches.

Second story contains front chamber, 13 feet 6 inches by 14 feet; study, 7 feet 6 inches by 9 feet 6 inches, and balcony; chamber over sitting room, 13x13 feet 6 inches, and one over dining room 11x12 feet 6 inches; servant's room, 9 feet 6 inches by 8 feet; bath room, 6 feet 6 inches by 10 feet, and closets in abundance.   Attic stairs when desired (always with 20-foot 4-inch posts), located over the three closets off from hall.   All pine finish.

MODIFICATIONS: The two different first floor plans show how a chamber and bath room can be had upon first floor or not.   A fire-place can be placed in dining room and sitting room.   In either plan design can be exteriorly changed and balcony dispensed with upon second story, front gable covering the entire hall full height.

Estimate cost of original design $2,000 to $2,600; as changed in other plan, with chamber and bath room first floor, $2,300 to $2,800.

See price list for cost of full plans, page vi.

The lowest estimate of cost is in accordance with price list of materal and labor as given on page v, and by comparing with your local prices, you can ascertain the cost of any of these buildings in your vicinity.

For changing shingles to clapboards on exterior of any design or reversing of plans, no extra charge will be made.

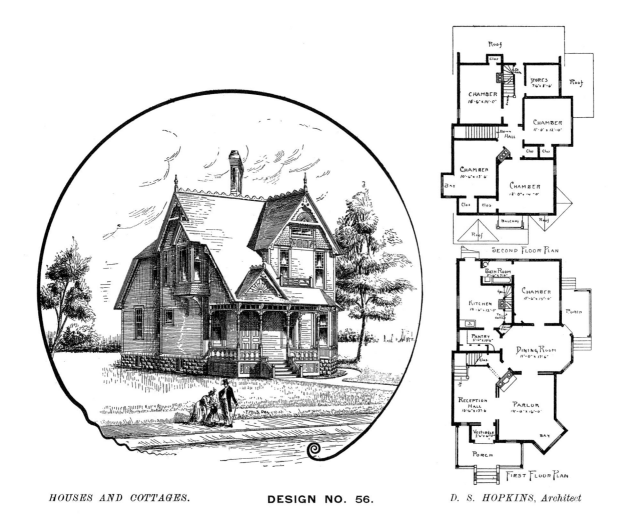

HOUSES AND COTTAGES. **DESIGN NO. 56.** *D. S. HOPKINS, Architect*

DESIGN NO. 56.

FRAME two story cottage. A very popular design for an inexpensive dwelling, considering the amount of room and conveniences it contains. Size, 35x50 feet, over all. Height of stories: First, 10 feet; second, 9 feet; cellar under entire house, 7 feet deep. Stone foundation to cellar bottom. Sides clapboarded; gables shingled. Shingled roof.

First story contains vestibule, 3 feet 6 inches by 6 feet; reception hall, 10 feet 6 inches by 13 feet 6 inches; parlor, 14x15 feet, with fire-place; dining room, 11x17 feet 6 inches; chamber, 11 feet 6 inches by 15 feet; kitchen, 10 feet 6 inches by 12 feet; pantry, 5x10 feet; bath room, 5 feet 6 inches by 7 feet 6 inches; back and front stairs; front and side porches.

Second story contains front chamber, 13x14 feet; side front bay chamber, 10 feet 6 inches by 13 feet 6 inches; chamber back of stairs, 10 feet 6 inches by 14 feet; side projecting chamber, 11x12 feet; store room, 7 feet 6 inches by 8 feet 6 inches. Hardwood finish for best rooms, first floor, and pine for balance. No plumbing, mantels, grates or heating.

MODIFICATIONS: Chamber can be used as dining room and bath room as pantry, and bath room put in place of present pantry or upon second floor where marked "store room." Back part can be carried up same height as main rear part and two more chambers provided for. Stairs can be made open all the way up if desired. By some changes in closets, second floor, a fire-place can be put in front chamber. Exterior can be changed. Estimate cost as here shown, $2,100 to $2,800.

See price list for cost of full plans, page vi.

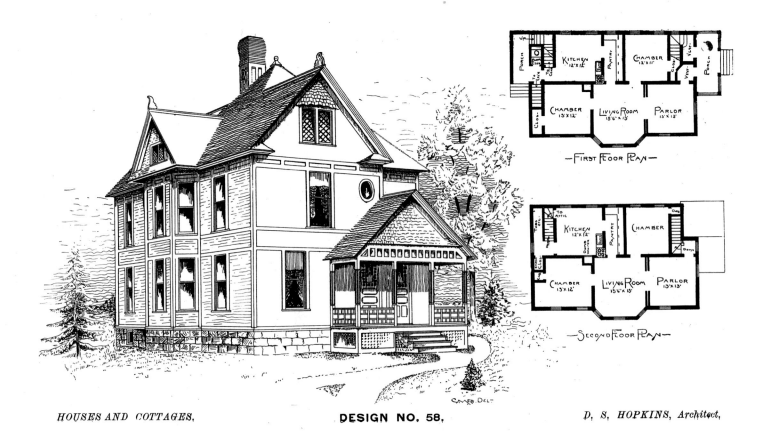

DESIGN NO. 58.

FRAME two-story and attic double flat tenement. Size, 29x56 feet over all. The entrance to both tenements is from front porch, one equally as good as the other. You enter a vestibule and go up stairs into parlor, and on first floor directly into parlor from vestibule. The arrangement of rooms is just the same upon both floors, except that second floor has the use of attic, where two or three chambers could be finished off if desired. The Heaps sanitary earth closet in supposed to be used in these tenements. Second floor has an independent rear stairs, down to rear porch, and from there to cellar; cellars are seperated by brick walls, the fuel will be kept there; and second floor tenement has a dumb waiter wood box running from wood cellar to kitchen, of size to hold a day's supply of wood. Height of stories: First, 9 feet; second, 9 feet, cellar under rear part. Stone foundation to cellar bottom at cellar; sides clapboarded, gables clapboarded and shingled. Shingle roof.

Both stories contain vestibule, 4x5 feet; parlor, 13x13 feet; living room, 13x15 feet 6 inches; front chamber, 11x12 feet; kitchen, 12x12 feet, pantry, 5x12 feet; rear chamber, 12x13 feet; closets to all chambers. Finished in pine throughout.

MODIFICATIONS: By extending house back length of porch first story, a bath room could be provided for upon both floors off from chamber, next to living room, so arranged by a passage way and door at inner end of bath room, that it can be used from chamber or living room. Dumb waiter to project into kitchen in that event.

Estimate cost as here shown, $2,000 to $2,500.

See price list for cost of full plans, page vi.

The lowest estimate of cost is in accordance with price list of material and labor as given on page v, and by comparing with your local prices, you can ascertain the cost of any of these buildings in your vicinity.

For changing shingles to clapboards on exterior of any design or reversing of plans, no extra charge will be made.

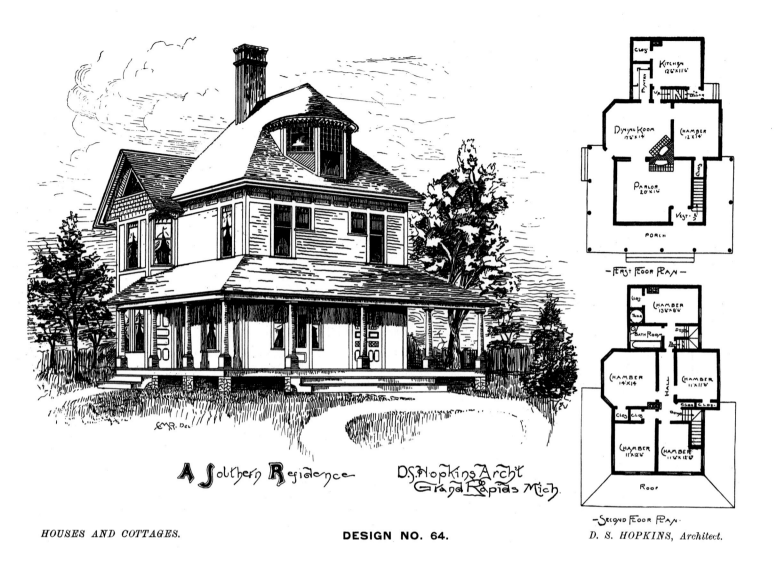

A Southern Residence   D.S. Hopkins Arch't
Grand Rapids Mich

- First Floor Plan -

- Second Floor Plan -

HOUSES AND COTTAGES.   **DESIGN NO. 64.**   *D. S. HOPKINS, Architect.*

DESIGN NO. 64.

THIS is a Southern style of house, but equally as good for a Northern house when plenty of porches are de-sired. Size, 38x56 feet over all. Frame two-story residence and high attic. Height of stories: First, 11 feet; second, 10 feet. Set on posts or piers; sides clapboarded; gables shingled. Shingle roof.

First story contains vestibule, 8 feet 6 inches by 4 feet, with stairs from same; parlor, 16x20 feet, with fire-place; dining room, 14x17 feet 6 inches, with fire-place; chamber, 12x14 feet; kitchen, 11 feet 6 inches by 12 feet 6 inches; pantry, 5x9 feet. Back stairs, kitchen closet, etc.

Second story contains two front chambers, 11x12 feet 6 inches each; octagon chamber, 14x14 feet and a chamber 11x11 feet 6 inches; servant's chamber, 8 feet 6 inches by 13 feet 6 inches; bath room, 6x7 feet 6 inches. Pine finish. No plumbing, mantels or grates.

MODIFICATIONS: Could be set on foundation and cellar put under to suit. A front stair hall and open stair case could be provided by partitioning off from parlor out to corner of chimney and a door to chamber if desired from hall. In this case this house is a good convenient house, North or South. A fire-place could be provided in cham-ber second floor.

Estimate cost as here shown, $2,000 to $2,500.

See price list for cost of full plans, page vi.

The lowest estimate of cost is in accordance with price list of material and labor as given on page v, and by comparing with your local prices you can ascertain the cost of any of these buildings in your vicinity.

For changing shingles to clapboards on exterior of any design or reversing of plans, no extra charge will be made.

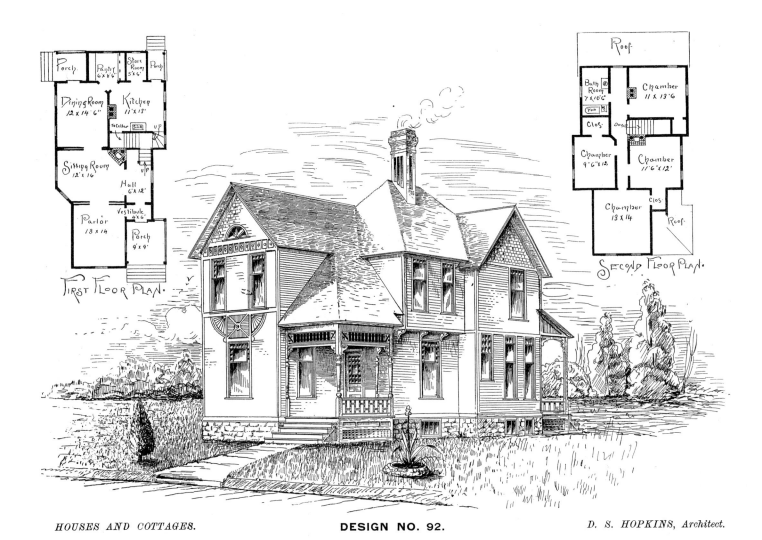

DESIGN NO. 92.

DESIGN NO. 92.

FRAME two story dwelling. Size, 26x50 feet. This is an enlargement of my $800 prize design, No. 10, Book 4, which is a great favorite, but as many wish a little more room I have shown how it can be had without much extra cost. Height of stories: First, 10 feet; second, 9 feet 6 inches. Cellar under all of house back of parlor. Stone foundation to cellar bottom 7 feet deep. First and second stories clapboarded, gables shingled and paneled. Shingle roof.

First story has front porch, 9x9 feet; also dining room and kitchen porches; vestibule, 4x6 feet; parlor, 13x14 feet; sitting room, 12x16 feet, with fire-place; hall, 6x12 feet, connecting with sitting room with large opening so that it is as part of same; stairs start from hall and are open up five steps, can there be closed off by a door or portiere, they are termed double acting stairs, as they are used from kitchen as well; dining room, 12x14 feet 6 inches; kitchen, 11x 13 feet; pantry, 6x8 feet 6 inches; and store room 5x6 feet, sink, cellar stairs, etc.

Second story contains four chambers, closets and bath room, no attic except for storage. All pine finish throughout. No plumbing, mantels, grates or heating.

MODIFICATIONS: Front porch can go across the front of main part. Front stairs can be open stairs and rear stairs built in store room off from kitchen. This would change chamber arrangement very slightly in landing of rear stairs. Dining room porch could be changed into conservatory opening from dining room.

Estimate cost as here shown, $1,600 to $2,000.

See price list for cost of full plans, page vi.

The lowest estimate of cost is in accordance with price list of material and labor as given on page v, and by comparing with your local prices you can ascertain the cost of any of these buildings in your vicinity.

For changing shingles to clapboards on exterior of any design or reversing of plans, no extra charge will be made.

First Floor Plan

Second Floor Plan

PARLOR 12'X15'6"

SITTING OR DINING ROOM 14'6"X15'

CHAMBER OR DINING ROOM 11'X14'6"

KITCHEN 12'6"X11'6"

PANTRY

PORCH

PORCH

CHAMBER 9'6"X14'

CHAMBER 12'X15'

HALL

CHAMBER 11'X14'

HOUSES AND COTTAGES,   DESIGN NO. 29.   D. S. HOPKINS, Architect

DESIGN NO. 29.

FRAME two-story cottage, rather attractive. Size, 26x43 feet. Height of stories: First, 9 feet 6 inches; second, 8 feet 6 inches; cellar under center part of building 7 feet deep. Stone foundation. Exterior sides clapboarded, gables paneled and shingled. Shingle roof.

First story contains hall, 6x11 feet 6 inches; parlor, 12x15 feet 6 inches; sitting or dining room, 13x14 feet 6 inches, with fire-place; chamber or dining room, 11x14 feet 6 inches; kitchen, 11 feet 6 inches by 12 feet 6 inches; pantry, 6x7 feet. Front and side porches, closets, etc., and double acting stairs.

Second story contains front chamber, 12x15 feet; side chamber, 9 feet 6 inches by 14 feet; side chamber, 11x14 feet, and closets to all chambers. Pine finish. No mantel or grate.

MODIFICATIONS: Cellar under whole house. Another kitchen can be built on back by changing porch and pantry and present kitchen by enlarging back, can be used as dining room. Rear part can be carried up and another chamber or bath room provided for.

Estimate cost as here shown, $1,400 to $1,700.

The lowest estimate of cost is in accordance with price list of material and labor as given on page v, and by comparing with your local prices, you can ascertain the cost of any of these buildings in your vicinity.

For changing shingles to clapboards on exterior of any design or reversing of plans, no extra charge will be made.

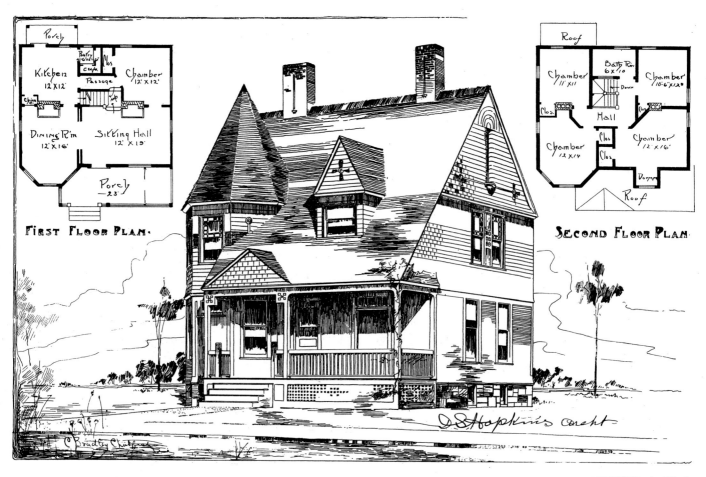

First Floor Plan.

Second Floor Plan.

DESIGN NO. 140.

FRAME two-story cottage. Size 30x32 feet over all. This design would make a good summer resort cottage as well as a permanent all-the-year house. Height of stories: first, 9 feet 6 inches; second, 8 feet. Stone foundation and cellar under the whole house 7 feet deep. First story sides clapboarded; second story shingles or clapboarding. Gables and roof shingles.

First story contains sitting hall, with fire-place and stair case, 12x19 feet; dining room, 12x16 feet, with fireplace; kitchen, 12x12 feet; pantry, 4 feet 6 inches by 5 feet 6 inches; chamber, 12x12 feet, with closet; large front porch, 8x22 feet.

Second story contains two front chambers, one 12x14 feet, and one 12x16 feet; side chamber, 11x11 feet; servant's room, 10 feet 6 inches by 12 feet; bath room, 5 feet 6 inches by 9 feet 6 inches, with closets to all chambers.

MODIFICATIONS: Hall could be cut off from sitting room 4 feet wide and stairs at end reversed, and have sitting room, 12x15 feet, with fire-place, same as now. Extra room can be built on for kitchen so as to enlarge present kitchen and make dining room of it. Fire-place in second story if desired.

Estimate cost as here shown, pine finish, no mantels, grates or heating, $1,400 to $1,800.

See price list for cost of full plans, page vi.

The lowest estimate of cost is in accordance with price list of material and labor as given on page v, and by comparing with your local prices, you can ascertain the cost of any of these buildings in your vicinity.

For changing shingles to clapboards on exterior of any design or reversing of plans, no extra charge will be made.

DESIGN NO. 169. *D. S. HOPKINS, Architect.*

DESIGN NO. 169.

FRAME two story dwelling. Size, 27x41 feet over all. Height of stories: First, 10 feet; second, 9 feet 6 inches. Stone foundation and cellar under whole house. First story clapboarded. Second story clapboards or shingles. Shingle gables. Shingle roof.

First story contains vestibule, 4x6 feet; reception or sitting hall, 13x14 feet (with fire-place and stair case); parlor or sitting room, 13x15 feet (with fire-place); dining room, 12x16 feet (with fire-place); kitchen, 10 feet 6 inches by 14 feet with closet, cupboards, etc. The stairs are double acting. From kitchen by two doors, and to cellar under same from hall. From reception hall you can reach all rooms and up stairs. Back of fire-places there is a fire-proof closet. Large front porch.

Second story contains two front chambers, one 13x15 feet 6 inches; one 13x14 feet 6 inches; two back; one 12x14 feet; one 10x14 feet, and closets to all.

MODIFICATIONS: House could be enlarged and another room added in rear to first and second stories, with rear stairs. A bath room could be arranged upon second story, by making some changes in closets, and using closet space for bath room.

Estimate cost as here shown, no mantels, grates or heating, pine finish, $1,300 to $1,800. Add for hard wood finish in three principal rooms and vestibule, including stairs as far as in sight from reception hall, $75.

See price list for cost of full plans, page vi.

The lowest estimate of cost is in accordance with price list of material and labor as given on page v, and by comparing with your local prices, you can ascertain the cost of any of these buildings in your vicinity.

For changing shingles to clapboards on exterior of any design or reversing of plans, no extra charge will be made.

DESIGN NO. 180.

FRAME two story cottage. Size, 33x42 feet over all. A cheap convenient square house. Height of stories: First, 9 feet; second, 8 feet 6 inches. Stone foundation and cellar under entire house 7 feet deep. First story clapboarded. Second story and gables shingles. Shingle roof.

First story contains vestibule, 5x8 feet and closet; hall, 7 feet 6 inches by 13 feet, with closed stair case from same with side hand rail; parlor, 11 feet 6 inches by 13 feet, with fire-place; sitting room, 13x14 feet; dining room, 12 feet 6 inches by 14 feet; pantry, 5 feet 6 inches by 10 feet 6 inches; kitchen, 12x14 feet. There is a passageway from kitchen to front hall by two doors and off from this passageway is a lavatory 3 feet 6 inches by 4 feet. Large front porch.

Second floor contains two front chambers, one 12x13 feet; one 13x14 feet; two in rear, one 11 feet 6 inches by 12 feet; one 10 feet 6 inches by 11 feet, aed plenty of closets; bath room, 6x9 feet; pine finish, no mantels, grates or heating.

MODIFICATIONS: Fire-place could be placed in sitting room and dining room if desired. Hard wood finish in principal rooms. Fire-place could be put in three chambers second floor if required.

Estimate cost as here shown, $1,700 to $2,000.

See price list for cost of full plans, page vi.

The lowest estimate of cost is in accordance with price list of material and labor as given on page v, and by comparing with your local prices, you can ascertain the cost of any of these buildings in your vicinity.
For changing shingles to clapboards on exterior of any design or reversing of plans, no extra charge will be made.

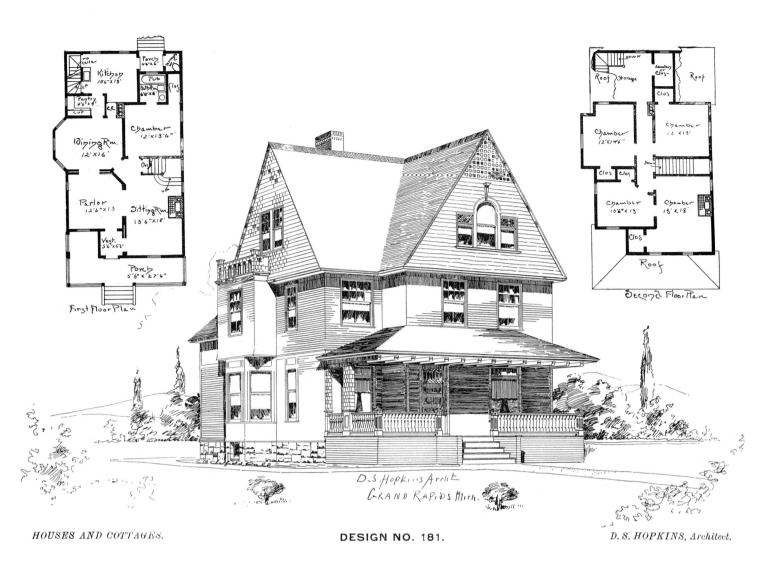

DESIGN NO. 181.

FRAME two-story cottage. Size 31x52 feet over all. A desirable double room front design. Height of stories: First, 9 feet 4 inches; second, 8 feet 2 inches. Stone foundation and cellar under dining room and chamber and rear part 7 feet deep. Arranged for furnace heating. First and second stories clapboarded. Gables shingled. Shingle roof.

First story contains vestibule 5 feet 6 inches by 6 feet; sitting hall, 13 feet 6 inches by 18 feet (with fire place); parlor, 12 feet 6 inches by 13 feet; dining room, 12x16 feet; chamber, 12x13 feet 6 inches with closet, and kitchen, 10 feet 6 inches by 13 feet; bath room, 6 feet 6 inches by 6 feet 6 inches; pantry, 4 feet 6 inches by 9 feet; servant's water closet off from rear porch. Rear and large front porch. Back and front stairs.

Second floor contains two front chambers in suite, one 13x18 feet; one 10 feet 6 inches by 13 feet; two back, one 12x14 feet 6 inches; and one 12x13 feet; closets, lavatory, 4x8 feet; storage, etc.

MODIFICATIONS: Fire place in chamber or dining room, also in one other chamber, second floor, if desired. Cellar under whole house divided into two parts. No plumbing, mantels, grates or heating. Plumbing costs $300. Hard wood for four rooms, including hard wood stairs over pine $100.

Estimate cost as here shown, $2,000 to $2,500.

See price list for cost of full plans, page vi.

The lowest estimate of cost is in accordance with price list of material and labor as given on page v, and by comparing with your local prices, you can ascertain the cost of any of these buildings in your vicinity.

For changing shingles to clapboards on exterior of any design or reversing of plans, no extra charge will be made.

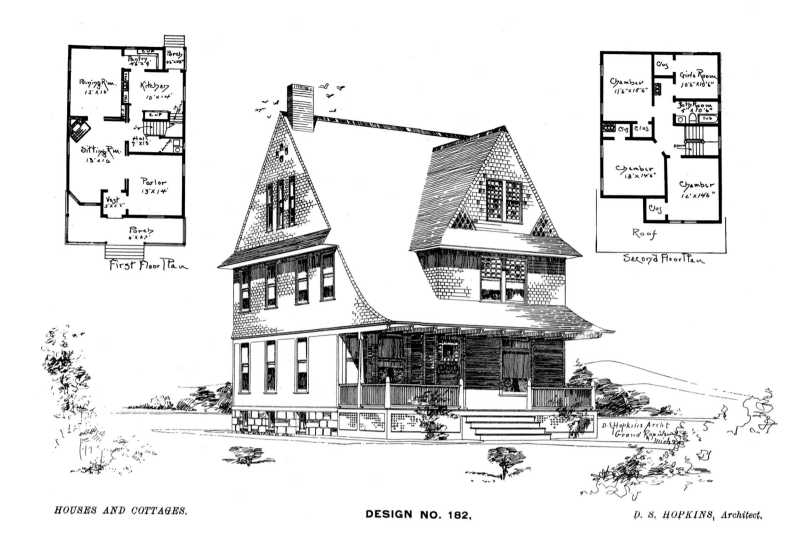

First Floor Plan

Second Floor Plan

DESIGN NO. 182.

DESIGN NO. 182.

FRAME two story cottage. Size, 28x45 feet over all. Height of stories: First, 9 feet 4 inches; second, 8 feet 2 inches. Cement bank shelf cellar under entire house 6 feet 6 inches deep. Stone foundation. First and second stories clapboarded. Gables and roofs shingels.

First story contains vestibule, 5x5 feet; sitting room, 13x16 feet; with fire-place; parlor, 13x14 feet; stair hall, 7x13 feet, with lavatory; dining room, 12x16 feet; kitchen, 10x14 feet, with cupboards; pantry, 4 feet 6 inches by 9 feet. Rear and large front porch.

Second story contains two front chambers, one 12x14 feet; one 12 feet 6 inches by 14 feet 6 inches; one rear, 11x15 feet 6 inches; one 10 feet 6 inches by 11 feet, with closets; bath room, 5x11 feet.

MODIFICATIONS: Fire-place in dining room, also in chamber second floor. House could be generally enlarged.

Estimate cost as here shown, pine finish, no plumbing, mantels, grates or heating, $1,600 to $1,800. Plumbing, $150. Hard wood for three rooms and hall, $85.

See price list for cost of full plans, page vi.

The lowest estimate of cost is in accordance with price list of material and labor as given on page v, and by comparing with your local prices you can ascertain the cost of any of these buildings in your vicinity.

For changing shingles to clapboards on exterior of any design or reversing of plans, no extra charge will be made.

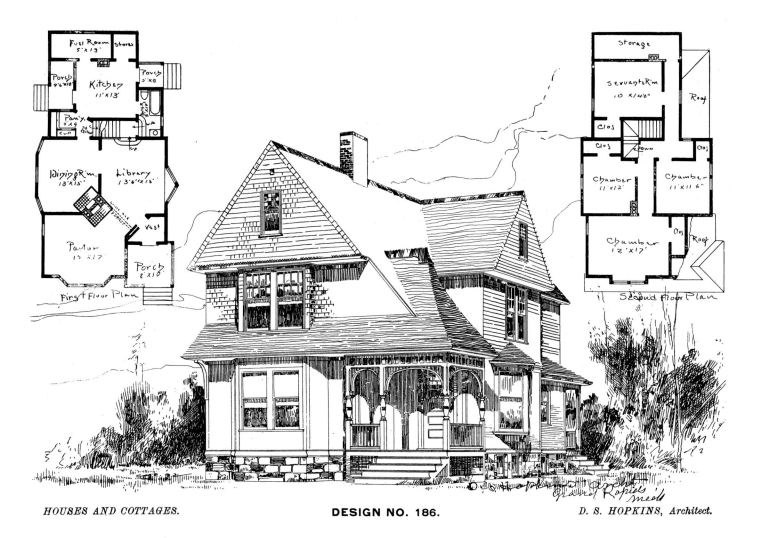

HOUSES AND COTTAGES.   **DESIGN NO. 186.**   *D. S. HOPKINS, Architect.*

DESIGN NO. 186.

FRAME two story cottage. Size, 30x52 feet over all. This is rather a peculiar arangement of floor plan, and yet one of merit. The parlor and library or sitting room are virtully one room; one fire-place does nicely for both and a grill finish and portiere can be provided for where shown if desired. The bath room is arranged off from side of kitchen with door from same, and also door from stair landing, making the bath room convenient from all parts of house, and also reducing the plumbing to a minimum in cost; or where one cent afford full plumbing a bath tub could be provided and water heated at stove, and carried in for bathing purposes.

First story contains vestibule, 5x6 feet; parlor, with bay, 12x17 feet; library or sitting room, 13 feet 6 inches by 15 feet, with bay and fire-place between the two; dining room, 13x15 feet, with fire-place and bay; pantry, 5x8 feet 6 inches; kitchen, 11x13 feet, with store closet and fuel room off from same, and porch each side; bath room 5x10 feet. Main stairs from library and to cellar from pantry. Large front porch.

Second story contains front chamber, 12x17 feet; and two back, one 11x12 feet; one 11x11 feet 6 inches, and servant's room, 10x14 feet 6 inches, and closets to all, storage, etc.

MODIFICATIONS: Cellar under entire house. Bath room could be changed to second story. Stairs could be turned around and library used as chamber by partitioning off same from parlor and vestibule. Another fire-place could be placed in chamber, second floor.

Estimate cost as here shown, no plumbing, mantels, grates or heating, pine interior finish, $1,000 to $1,400.

See price list for cost of full plans, page vi.

DESIGN NO. 187.

D. S. HOPKINS, Architect.

DESIGN NO. 187.

FRAME two story dwelling. Size, 40x44 feet over all. Height of stories: First, 10 feet; second, 9 feet 6 inches. Stone foundation and cellar under entire house 7 feet deep. First and second stories clapboarded. Gables shingled. Shingle roof. This is an odd arrangement, a little off from the usual, but think upon investigation you will say it is a pleasant and convenient combination. It opens up so pleasant and the first view on entering hall will be fine. The stair case, landing and bay is rich in general effect, with fire-places and glimpses into the adjoining rooms, all giving richness and grandeur to the first impression.

First story contains vestibule, 5x5 feet 6 inches; hall, averaging 8x20 feet, with fire-place and stair case, bay, etc.; parlor, 12 feet 6 inches by 14 feet; sitting room or library, 13 feet 6 inches by 14 feet, with bay and fire-places; dining room, 12x16 feet, with fire-place; off from dining room and adjoining vestibule is a toilet room with wash bowl; kitchen, 10x13 feet 6 inches; pantry, 7x7 feet; entry or storage place, 6x7 feet 6 inches; rear stairs from same and place for refrigerator; rear porch and large front porch.

Second story contains three front chambers; one 12x12 feet; one 11 feet 6 inches by 12 feet; one 12x13 feet, with fire-place; servant's room, 8x10 feet 6 inches, and closets to all chambers; attic stairs.

MODIFICATIONS: A fire-place in parlor and one in chamber, directly over two chambers in front second story instead of three. Laundry in basement.

Estimate cost as here shown, hard wood first floor, principal rooms. Pine, balance of finish. Plumbing complete. No mantels, grates or heating. $2,800 to $3,300.

See price list for cost of full plans, page vi.

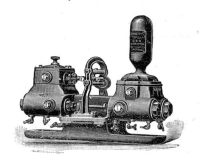

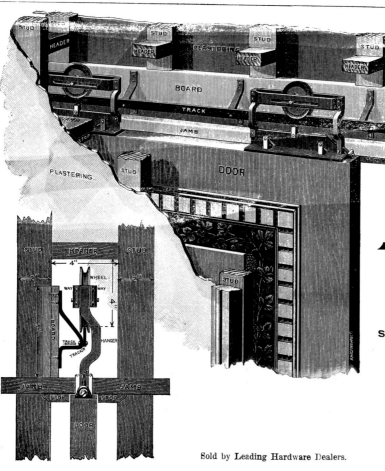